ILLUMINING SHAME, ANGER, and FORGIVENESS

TRANSFORMATIVE WISDOM SERIES

THE TRANSFORMATIVE WISDOM SERIES engages the themes of spiritual, personal, and societal transformation, bringing to bear the timeless wisdom of the Eastern Orthodox Church and the cumulative wisdom of contemporary Western psychotherapies.

Also by the author:

- ✎ *Traditions of the Healing Church: Exploring the Orthodox Faith*

Books by Deacon Stephen Muse, PhD:

- ✎ *Raising Lazarus: Integral Healing in Orthodox Christianity* (Editor & contributor)
- ✎ *When Hearts Become Flame: An Eastern Approach to the Dia-Logos of Pastoral Counseling*
- ✎ *Being Bread*
- ✎ *Treasure in Earthen Vessels: Prayer and the Embodied Life*

Illumining
Shame, Anger, and
Forgiveness

Nun Katherine Weston, MA, LMHC
Foreword by Deacon Stephen Muse, PhD

Weston Counseling, LLC

Publications
Indianapolis, Indiana
2018

Printed with the blessing of His Grace
✣ Longin
Serbian Orthodox Bishop of the Diocese
of New Gracanica and Midwestern America

Copyright © 2018 by Nun Katherine Weston

Cover icon: Expulsion from Paradise painted by John Rigby for the Saints Constantine and Elena Orthodox Church in Indianapolis.

About the Weston Counseling, LLC, logo: The nautilus shell presents a pattern of growth that God has used from the smallest sea creatures to the greatest cosmic nebulae. It is a metaphor for psychological healing: We cycle through themes, but at a greater breadth of healing each time. The Cross is our spiritual healing. At the center of both is a pearl— Christ Himself.

Weston Counseling, LLC, Publications
ISBN-13: 978-0-9983906-3-5

BISAC: REL012110
Religion / Christian Life / Spiritual Warfare

Contents

Foreword

READING THIS DELIGHTFUL tapestry of reflections, I was reminded of what I liked in Nun Katherine Weston's presentations when I first heard her speak a decade earlier in Sarasota, Florida and again in Chicago at International Conferences of Orthodox Christian psychotherapists. She is concise, orderly, and clear. Her themes are well-researched, drawing both from the Holy Fathers and from modern psychotherapists, as well as her own experiences and reflections as a monastic amplified by a decade of hearing the stories of suffering persons in her counseling practice.

The universal themes of shame, anger, and forgiveness presented here are the first of several planned in a Transformative Wisdom Series devoted to exploring "spiritual, personal, and societal transformation" by engaging in a fruitful dialogue between "the timeless wisdom of the Eastern Orthodox Church and the cumulative wisdom of contemporary Western psychotherapies." I believe she succeeds in honoring both domains without confusing or conflating them as she attempts to offer practical counsel and insight into the above-mentioned three areas vital to human development.

Created as stand-alone essays, the themes of this volume gain their unity from the original shame of the ancestral curse at the root of human separation from God and one another; moving through the power of anger to injure and to protect, culminating in a fascinating final chapter on religious zeal and forgiveness.

The volume begins with the ontological recognition that in the beginning, before communion with God was broken, Adam and Eve were "naked and unashamed." She then explores the nature of shame, broadening the discussion by exploring the impact of slavery, trauma, and child abuse, to further reveal the impact shame has in human development.

Next, she draws on Patristic discernment of healthy and unhealthy anger to illumine the essential role of feeling in the spiritual struggle for salvation, using insights of modern psychology to help illumine healthy ascetical efforts from those that distort and cripple the soul.

Finally, she explores forgiveness through the parable of the Prodigal Son. The relationship between the religious strivings of the Pharisee (or *Perushim* which she points out in Hebrew, means "separated") and the capacity for mercy and forgiveness, are explored through the story of the elder brother who distinguishes himself from his "prodigal brother," angrily rejecting the Father's mercy toward the latter's repentance.

I was edified and stimulated by her reflections and scholarship in this volume and found myself returning to one of Dag Hammarskjöld's observations in his book *Markings.* The respected and widely traveled former Swedish U.N. Secretary General elucidated the seeming paradox inherent to the human religious striving:

> Except in faith nobody is humble. The mask of weakness or of Phariseeism is not the naked face of humility. And except in faith nobody is proud. The vanity displayed in all its varieties by the spiritually immature is not pride. To be, in faith, both humble and proud: that is to *live,* to know that in God I am nothing, but that God is in me.[1]

Mother Katherine's reflections reinforced for me the often overlooked fact that even the disciples suffered from the same tendency as the Pharisees. They too were actively creating an identity out of comparing themselves to others. The Apostle Peter confessed that in his zeal: He told Jesus *"Even if all these fall away because of you I will not!"* (Mt. 26:33). Hammarskjöld continues,

> Humility is just as much the opposite of self-abasement as it is of self-exaltation. To be humble is *not to make comparisons* [my emphasis]. Secure in its reality, the self is neither better nor worse, bigger nor smaller, than anything else in the universe. It *is*—is nothing, yet at the same time one with everything. It is in this sense that humility is absolute self-effacement.[2]

Recognizing none of us can separate ourselves from the humanity in which we are all made and that "humility is genuine only when Christ is present"[3] we do well to cry out, *Lord Jesus Christ have mercy on me a sinner!* From the embrace of repentance arising from communion with Christ and all whom He loves, we find ourselves yet again naked . . . but no longer ashamed.

November 13, 2017
The feast of St. John Kochurov
of Chicago

The Rev. Deacon Stephen Muse, PhD
Director of Education and Counselor Training
and Clergy-in-Kairos Program
at the Pastoral Institute in Columbus, Georgia

NOTES

[1] Hammarskjöld, Dag. (1983). *Markings*, (Sjöberg, L. & Auden, W. H., Trans.). New York: Ballantine, p. 75.

[2] Hammarskjöld, Dag. (1959). *Markings*, 4, 174, as cited in Froehlich, M. (2008). *Political ethics and the United Nations: Dag Hammarskjöld as Secretary-General*. New York: Routledge, p. 71.

[3] Papacios, (Archimandrite) Arsenie. (2011). "Eternity hidden in the moment." *The Orthodox Word*, No. 281. Platina, CA: St. Herman of Alaska Brotherhood, p. 289.

PREFACE

As I was first approaching Orthodoxy in the early 1980s, friends in my faith community were reading a book called *Psychology as Religion: The Cult of Self-Worship* by Paul C. Vitz. However nuanced the author's views may have been, my take-away from the book discussions was that we, as Christians, needed to stay away from psychology. The title alone was enough to give that impression, so I continued my search for healing of the soul through strictly Orthodox texts. "Psychology," of course, means the knowledge and science of the soul, and the Orthodox Church has had true, spiritual psychology and soul therapy from the beginning. On the other hand, I persistently struggled to apply what was written for other generations and cultures and conditions.

Therefore, seeing no better recourse, I began to explore and draw from psychology's therapeutic techniques and clinical experience. However, I abstained from its vision of the nature of man and wellness, which do diverge significantly from a traditional, Christian understanding.

A cogent reason for my—and other Christians'—caution was that early psychotherapists pathologized faith, although this view softened over time. It began with Freud, born in 1856 to a Jewish family in Austria. He eventually left the faith of his fathers. Decades later Carl Rogers (born 1902) and Rollo May (born 1909), both products of a Midwestern Christian upbringing, studied at the liberal Union Theological Seminary in New

York. Leaving faith behind, they went on, respectively, to develop humanistic and existential models for healing. Moving ahead another generation, Ana-Maria Rizzuto (born 1932) is a devout Roman Catholic and an Argentinian analyst who analyzed Freud's rejection of God. Baptist minister Harville Hendrix (born 1935) has a dual doctorate in religion and psychology from the University of Chicago Divinity School. He developed a model of couples therapy that is quite compatible with Orthodox teaching. I select these five names to illustrate a gradual change, such that psychology and Christian faith have become more comfortable conversation partners. The conversation is taking place across national and denominational lines.

Some 20 years after *Psychology as Religion*, Dr. Vitz published a more optimistic view on psychology entitled "Psychology in Recovery." He says:

> I was a public and rather harsh critic of much popular psychology in my first publications in the 1970s and '80s. I stand by those views. But much has changed, and changed (to my surprise) for the better. Particularly in the therapeutic discipline, and specifically in the past generation, a new and salutary understanding of what psychotherapy is and is not has been developed.

Various conferences on Orthodox Christianity and psychology have now been meeting for years. I was privileged to present papers at two of these. More importantly, I was enriched by hearing other presenters who had dual vocations as physician, psychiatrist, psychologist, or therapist, and Orthodox priest or deacon. The conversation which I stepped into apologetically in 2002, I see now, fifteen years later, publically validated by many trustworthy voices in the Orthodox Church. Likewise new books on how Orthodoxy can be served by psychology are published regularly.

In 2003 I began my seminary degree program in pastoral care and counseling in what turned out to be a five-year journey. In this volume, the first essay and the second two essays bracket that journey. Through writing the first essay on generational shame I slowly began to realize my own calling to pastoral psychotherapy. The second essay, "Hope for Anger," is distilled from my master's thesis on anger management in the early Church and cognitive behavioral therapy. The third essay was written just a year before graduation. It features a group dynamics approach to the issues of forgiving and welcoming the returning "prodigal."

I wish to express my gratitude to Monk Cosmas (Shartz), writer and translator, who kindly made editorial comments on all three essays. He often pushed me to research my points further when he thought more evidence would speak for itself. Thank you to Fr. Dn. Stephen Muse, PhD, for his inspiration shared through presentations, authorship and, now, contributing the foreword. My appreciation again goes to editorial readers Matushka Margaret Bauman and seminary student Xenia Lundeen. Without the help of my patient monastic sisters at St. Xenia's in Indianapolis, my books would never come to fruition. Thank you to inspired iconographer John Rigby for again contributing a cover icon.

    As always, my heartfelt appreciation goes to the Brotherhood of St. Moses the Black and all affiliated with it. My talks delivered at their conferences in Kansas City, Missouri; Darien Illinois; and Springfield, Missouri form the basis for this volume. The brotherhood strives "to equip Orthodox Christians for the ministry of racial reconciliation and to share the Orthodox Christian faith with African Americans and people of color."

September 24, 2017
The glorification of St. Xenia of St. Petersburg,
Patron Saint of my monastic community

Nun Katherine Weston

First Essay, 2002:
Freedom from Generational Shame

Psychologists since the time of Freud have been studying guilt—the gnawing feeling that we have acted badly—and its role in our lives. In 1987, Daniel Goleman began a *New York Times* article with this bit of irony:

> Psychologists, admittedly chagrined and a little embarrassed, are belatedly focusing on shame, a prevalent and powerful emotion, which somehow escaped rigorous scientific examination until now.

Shame feels similar to guilt, but it has more to do with who we are than what we do. He continues: "Shame is emerging, in the view of some, as a 'master emotion' that influences all the others" (Goleman, 1987, sec. 3, p. 1). I've been pleased to discover that Christian therapists—Protestant, Catholic, and Orthodox—are now wrestling with this topic. Some are also including the Bible as an important point of reference.

This essay discusses shame from the point of view of the Bible and other familiar Orthodox sources, as well as modern psychology and social commentary. It begins with an overview of what it is and then explores its causes, its significance, its manifestations, and its resolution.

Shame in the Bible

The Bible speaks about shame from beginning to end. I was surprised to find in the concordance that there were six times as many references to shame as to guilt in the Scriptures. The whole drama of the fall and salvation of man is couched in terms of shame, both in the Bible, and in the Divine Services of the Church. When we pray for salvation for our souls we say, "Let us not who put our hope in Thee be put to shame," and similar phrases. When we pray for deliverance from the demons we say, "let mine enemies quickly be put to shame."

The story of shame starts in Genesis. We are told that our first parents in Paradise were *naked, ... and were not ashamed* (Gen. 2:25). "Not ashamed" are the only words used to describe the paradisal state of their souls. Surely they were also joyful, peaceful, grateful; "not ashamed," though, seems to sum up that blissful state and imply all other blessings. After their fall through disobedience their shame is described by their actions—they hid and they blamed (see Gen. 3:7-13). Both the Church and psychotherapy recognize hiding and blaming as symptoms of shame.

Now we will draw on a traditional, patristic view of Genesis to enhance our understanding of shame. Our first parents were created to be immortal. They were wise beyond any human comparison. They did not suffer from hunger, thirst, heat, cold, fatigue, disease, injury, and did not need to suffer death. Their eating did not produce waste, and they lived as virgins (see Rose, 2000). But Adam and Eve disobeyed God, and fell from all the goodness which had freely been given to them. For the first time they experienced shame. Shame is an emotion; it is also a state of being at odds with ourselves and with God. Shame says, "I have fallen from the good state in which I was created. I, who was just under the angels, am now like one of the beasts. The whole creation is cursed for my sake. I see my sin exposed—I deserve to be rejected by God and cast away from His presence."

What a painful feeling of rupture and needless devastation! In the grips of burning shame, we can hardly even stand to look at ourselves, at the exposure of our shortcomings.

Shame not only makes us hide from God, and each other, but we hide our shamed state from ourselves by a myriad of smoke screens. The Church calls this hiding self-delusion. And it calls the smoke screens "the passions." From its vantage point, psychology also calls this hiding self-delusion. And it calls the smoke screens "defense mechanisms." I use the term "smoke screen" as a broad metaphor and do not mean to imply that the passions *are* defense mechanisms, but rather that we can hide from ourselves behind either.

The ultimate cause of shame, as we have seen, is the sin of our first parents. Unlike the Western Church, which teaches that we inherit the guilt of Adam, the Eastern Church teaches that we inherit the shame of Adam. As the canon for the feast of Theophany tells us,

> The Maker saw in the obscurity of sin, in bonds that
> knew no escape,
> The man whom He had formed with His own hand.
> Raising him up, He laid him on his shoulders,
> And now in abundant floods He washes him clean
> From the ancient shame of Adam's sinfulness [M. Mary & Ware, 1990, pp. 372 – 373].

Shame in human development

So FAR, EVERYTHING WE HAVE SAID about shame seems negative, but actually there is healthy shame, and there is unhealthy shame. We begin to see its significance for us in terms of human development. Our sense of shame appears around the age of two. We learn the distinction that certain things are private, such as our hygienic activities—we learn boundaries. This is an important, positive lesson. The capacity for shame develops before guilt, and before rational thinking. For this reason our early lessons about shame become part of our deepest sense of self, and are hard to revise if they have been contaminated by poisonous shame.

All our emotions are psychic energy—the energy of the soul. They are reactions given by God to help move us to make good responses to the situations around us. For instance, joy moves us to praise God. Fear moves us out of harm's way. Interest moves us to study and to work. When we have completed our response, then the emotion is resolved. Our heart moves on to something else. Shame in small, healthy doses tells us to correct our mistakes—to stop, recognize our human limitations, and proceed with prudence. If the feeling is rational, it can resolve itself in wisdom and insight. Here is a perspective on healthy shame from *Healing the Shame that Binds You* by John Bradshaw:

> It is necessary to have the feeling of shame if one is to be truly human. Shame is the emotion which gives us permission to be human. Shame tells us of our limits. Shame keeps us in our human boundaries, letting us know we can and will make mistakes, and that we need help. Our shame tells us we are not God. Healthy shame is the psychological foundation of humility. It is the source of spirituality [Bradshaw, 1988, p. vii].

But in large doses, shame becomes poisonous. Rather than telling us to *correct* ourselves, it tells us that we are *incorrigible*. It is that shamed sense of self which we constantly seek to drown out—the feeling is irrational and so there is no way to resolve it. For example, if I feel rationally ashamed and guilty because of a thoughtless remark, that will prompt me to seek forgiveness and to watch my tongue in the future. The guilt is resolved by making amends, and the shame is resolved by a firm decision not to repeat that mistake. Many of us have examples from our student days of things that made us irrationally ashamed. Here's one of mine: I remember feeling painfully and irrationally ashamed of being a good student. I was afraid that boys would reject me for seeming smarter than they were. What moral lesson could I learn from that? Occasionally I would attempt to resolve the shame by playing to lose in a competitive game. In this case, my shame made me hide my real self in relationship with others. With deeper shame, we try to escape the pain by hiding self from self. It is in this sense that shame becomes a powerful energy of avoidance—the avoidance of truth and reality about ourselves and our relationships. Bradshaw continues:

> Toxic shame is unbearable and always necessitates a cover-up, a false self. Since one feels his true self is defective and flawed, one needs a false self which is not defective and flawed. *Once one becomes a false self, one ceases to exist psychologically.* To be a false self is to cease being an authentic human being. The process of false self-formation is what Alice Miller calls "soul murder." As a false self, one tries to be more than human or less than human [pp. vii—viii].

"Soul murder," as Alice Miller so aptly calls it, is exactly what happened at the time of the original fall. God warned Adam that if he ate of the tree of the knowledge of good and evil, he would die. Adam lived in the flesh for a considerable time (see Gen. 5:5), yet there is no contradiction here. The immediate consequence of his sin was the death of his soul—the departure of the Holy Spirit from it. Through his lack of humility, he passed a legacy of shame and spiritual death down through the generations even to our present time. That leads us to contemplate the spiritual effects of shame next.

The spiritual effects of shame

HEALTHY SHAME WAS ANTICIPATED in the Old Testament righteous ones, but it is truly made possible by Christ's Incarnation and Baptism for our sake. Healthy shame is modeled by the Prodigal Son. That shame says, "I have fallen from grace, ungrateful as I am. I deserve to be rejected by God, but He is full of mercy and loving-kindness. I trust in His mercy, and dare to pray to Him with hope!" Our unhealthy shame says, "Don't look at me—I'm a mistake! I have a hole in my soul and I should never have been born. If people really knew how I was inside, they would hate and reject me." In other words, healthy shame still remembers that we are God's creation and that He loves us. We were created good, but have become mud-covered and diseased. We need cleansing and healing, not discarding. Unhealthy shame makes us feel that we, our family, or group have a defect that others do not share. That we have a hopelessly bad nature that cannot be fixed, cured, or changed. Again, healthy shame is the foundation of humility. Here is an example of healthy shame from the book *Unseen Warfare*—a repentant sinner is counseled to pray in these words:

> "O Lord, my God! I have done this because I am what I am and so nothing can be expected of me but such transgressions or even worse, if Thy grace does not help me and I am left to myself alone. I grieve over what I have done, especially because my life has no righteousness responding to Thy care of me, but I continue to fall and fall. Forgive me and give me the strength not to offend Thee again and in no way to digress from Thy will. For I zealously wish to work for Thee, to please Thee and be obedient to Thee in all things" [St. Theophan, 1978, p. 279].

This humble sinner recognizes that all good is borrowed from God, and so expects nothing good to come out of himself unaided. He is not afraid to look frankly at his failings and shortcomings, and is not scandalized by them. He does not get obsessed with them. After offering his repentance to God, he feels confident of forgiveness and goes on with life. He doesn't say, "how could I ever have done such a horrible thing! I'm really not that kind of person." (Or "I'm hopelessly that kind of person!") Squarely shouldering the healthy awareness of shame is a big part of carrying our cross and following Christ. It helps us not to judge and disparage our neighbor.

There is a profound state of imbalance and loss of perspective that is characteristic of the false self in fallen man. Our fall, the tasting of the tree of knowledge, opened us up to the experience of both good and evil, but tragically left us still without discernment. As we became coarse and material in our fallen nature, we became confused about the issues of pleasure and pain, good and evil. This undiscerning condition is so severe that the Church counsels us never to trust ourselves—our thoughts, our motives, our instincts, our judgments. The Church calls the false self the "old man." It is a death-like sleep of the soul that causes us to identify ourselves with our lower nature and our senses. It causes us to side with the irrational, sensual will, and not the higher, godly will. It is that false self which begins to wash away in baptism, and is the very reason that we must be born again.

In one of his homilies, St. Nikolai Velimirović further explains:

> There is a trinity in the interior heaven of man, which must become not just an association, but a unity, that he may be blessed both in this world and in that which is to come; that is the unity of mind, heart and will. While these three are only in association, man is at war with his own three parts and the heavenly Trinity [1985, p. 33].

In the fallen state, the mind, the heart, and the will are out of balance with each other, at war with each other and with God. Poisonous shame encourages us to feel ashamed of some parts of our threefold make-up—sometimes to the point of not acknowledging that they are there, and to over-identify with other parts. For instance, a person could be over-identified with the mind, and ashamed of his feelings, or some of his feelings. A Western upbringing tends to give the sense that some feelings are intrinsically good and some are intrinsically bad. Love, joy, and excitement are "good," while sorrow, anger, and fear are "bad." In truth, all that God put into our make-up is good, but we need discernment—we have to know when and how to use it. If we are brought up to believe that all anger is bad, then how will we be angry against the demons and our passions? If we believe that all fear is bad, how will we develop fear of God? If we believe that all sorrow is bad, how will we sorrow for our sins and repent?

The manifestations of toxic shame

As WE HAVE DEFINED SHAME, both healthy and unhealthy, and looked at its significance, we have done so in universal terms. To look at the many manifestations of toxic shame, we will resume our creation story, and then move on to particular circumstances. The first beings to be shamed were the spirits who fell from heaven due to their over-weaning pride. Man was created a little lower than the angels in order to grow and to fill the void left by the fall of a third of them or more, according to some traditional Church sources. God shamed the demons in an ultimate way by casting them down from heaven, and from all that is good. The demons try to retaliate by shaming God.

Shame for a creature is one thing—shame for God, impossible of course, would mean something entirely different. Shame for a creature results from unwisely choosing to trust the creation rather than the Creator—it means being cast away from God's presence. Shame for God would mean proving that He was unwise in His counsels, fallible in His foreknowledge, foolish in His generosity. In particular, it would mean showing that He had made a tremendous mistake in creating man to replace the fallen angels.

Tradition tells us that the demonic ranks are motivated by consuming and unquenchable envy. They try to tempt us night and day to prove that God was foolish to ever create us, and to prove that human beings, like the demons, are inherently enemies of God. In this pursuit, they are constantly blaming us before God, ourselves, and each other. In tormenting us they feel that they somehow ease their own torment. That is why the shameless ones provoke in our hearts the feeling that we are a mistake—that we shouldn't have been born. If we ever feel this way we need to know that the demons are tormenting the wound of the ancestral sin in us. They want to provoke us to blaspheme our Creator Who formed us to share in His goodness and bliss.

We mentioned earlier that shame causes hiding and blaming. So far, we have looked at the response of hiding, but we have said little about blaming. The nature of shame is such that the feeling of it can be shifted from one individual or group to another. The demons proudly teach us to participate in their ruse of shifting the hurt of shame onto others. They take great delight if we begin to grumble and to blame God for our miseries, or if we dull our distress by gloating about our supposed superiority over our neighbor. This could be moral superiority—a feeling of self-righteousness, or physical superiority—greater strength, or mental superiority—greater intelligence. We may also resort to the inverse superiority of feeling that we are the worst at something—the most delinquent, the most rejected and unloved, the worst failure. Still having the log in our own eye, we try to take the speck out of our neighbor's eye (cf. Mt. 7:3–5). We blame and judge our neighbor for our own unacknowledged faults and desires, which some therapists like to call our "shadow traits." Family relationships, racial and caste relationships, ethnic and national relationships—in fact all relationships—involve rituals either for maintaining a balance of shame or transferring shame.

Here is a simple example of maintaining the balance—a friend was with me in the monastery kitchen. As I finished the dishes, I looked down at my faded, black work habit and remarked that it was full of stains and grease spots. My friend was nicely dressed, but she immediately began pointing out invisible stains on her own clothing, too. She tactfully brought herself down to my level so that I wouldn't feel embarrassed. My heart felt lightened because of her kind gesture.

Conversely, if someone has criticized you, you may have noticed an insurmountable urge to find some "helpful" criticism to offer him in return. These are the little exchanges we are involved in every day. But they illustrate our ancestral wound—our fall and our subsequent search for balance.

Here is an example of how we begin to transfer shame to others—I went to fill up my car at a time when the gas prices were fluctuating wildly. The cashier made me feel really stupid for not knowing in advance how much it would cost to fill the tank. Next thing I knew, I was hunting in my mind for an excuse to chew out someone else, in order to relieve my own stinging embarrassment. Yelling, put-downs, or any abusive behavior will make the victim feel shamed. Why? In reality, the person who behaves abusively ought to be the one to feel ashamed of himself. But society teaches us to believe that we deserve what we get according to a this-worldly sense of the fairness of the universe—if we are treated shamefully we feel ashamed (see Matsakis, 1998). We learn to assess our worth from how others treat and see us. We learn who we are first from our parents and those in our families, then from those in society around us. Our sense of identity comes from agreeing with the most important people in our life about who and what we are or should be.

SHAME IN HISTORY

Shame in the practice of slavery

BEYOND THE FAMILY, the transference of shame in society has happened through the universal practice of slavery. From as far back as sociologists can trace history, it has always been there. Slavery seems to have its genesis in making the slave the carrier of toxic shame. He begins as a conquered warrior. He is ashamed because he couldn't defend himself or his women or his tribe. Then he is given a different name, distinctive dress or haircut, or some other mark. He must shoulder the work which his master scorns, and he has no recourse against the ridicule of society (see Patterson, 1982). Or again, he begins as a debtor who cannot feed his family. He shamefacedly sells himself into bondage and passes a growing debt onto his children and his children's children. The legacy of debt becomes a legacy of shame as the "free" people mock, cheat, and abuse them. Looking at American history, Dr. Aphrodite Matsakis, an Orthodox psychologist and author, discusses this transfer of shame in terms of "shadow traits":

> Many of our racial stereotypes originated in the need to project the shadow traits away from ourselves onto a distinct group. Hence, white slave owners made much of the unbridled sexuality of their African-American slaves, when in reality it was the white slave owners who were taking sexual advantage of their slaves. They projected their own uncontrolled lust onto their victims, calling them "seductive" or "oversexed" or

"immoral," when the problem wasn't the sexual desires of the slaves, but the sexual desires of the slave owners [1998, p. 77].

In every slave culture the bondwomen are raped, and their children are born into slavery. This is not an anomaly of American history but, rather, the norm.

Rape is one of the most standard procedures to ensure that women feel totally shamed and submissive (see Patterson, 1991 & Cotton, 1998). We can gain insight into how it works from Solzhenitsyn's *Gulag Archipelago*. He describes how Soviet prison guards used to deal with the hunger strikes of the political prisoners by force feeding, which he likens to rape in that it is a violation of the will. He observes that a person's will has to be violated only once in this way to induce a state of apathy, because he is made to feel like his own betrayer. The nerves of the stomach, or any other part of the body, cannot tell the source of stimulation. They register pleasure on a purely organic level. On the other hand, the heart and mind can react with strong disgust to things which are morally degrading and sinful. To make a person feel intense disgust and physical pleasure at the same time is to rip his soul in two. I wonder if there is a more shaming or demonically inspired thing one person can do to another than to accentuate the disharmony, originally caused by the fall, between the trinity of the mind, the heart, and the will. Or the trinity of the spirit, the soul, and the body.

Perhaps a very limited, non-traumatic example would provide the best illustration of that dynamic. Some years ago I was sitting in a hospital waiting room. The TV, tagged with a big, handwritten note: *Do not change the channel*, was inescapable. I waited for six hours using my prayer rope, but with nothing to read, nothing else to occupy my mind, and with that inane TV blaring in front of me. To escape boredom, I tasted the entertainment. I found it debasing and disrespectful to the guests on the show and to the institution of marriage. Husbands were subjected to a lie detector test publicly, in front of an audience, in an attempt to resolve marital conflicts. Yet my eyes, ears, and brain experienced some pleasure in being stimulated, in spite of the undesired content. Inside my soul was howling. I was angry with myself for watching, but too weak with boredom to resist.

Shame and needs

ABUSE IN FAMILIES may have something in common with that waiting room experience. Perhaps the abuse is verbal—it is shaming, but on the other hand, being yelled at is a form of attention. In the case of children, they become torn between the conflicting needs for attention and safety—some will sacrifice attention for safety, and some, safety for attention. Either way, the unmet need causes them shame. Because our natures provide for us to learn types of behavior that meet our needs, that sort of conflict may teach us to act in ways that encourage abuse or neglect, and it becomes a vicious cycle.

Our nature is equipped for survival—if we are unable to meet a need well, we will choose to meet it poorly rather than not at all. Later, the opportunity may arise to fulfill it in a better way but then, with difficulty, we have to unlearn unconscious habits. It's difficult to change because our habitual solution is bound up with our sense of identity—who we are. It's bound up with the creation of a false self that we spoke of earlier. Once our identity is formed we constantly seek to affirm it, even if it causes us shame. To admit, if only to ourselves and God, that we were wrong about who and what we thought we were, brings up even more powerful feelings of shame.

Our needs themselves are humbling. An angel, being immortal, has no survival needs—he lives by the presence of God alone. That is exactly how we were originally created, and how

God wants us to become, by virtue of spiritual rebirth. All the daily survival needs we have are as a result of the fall. The obligation to work to fulfill our needs is a result of the fall. Wealth and poverty are a result of the fall. God gave us the penance of neediness and hard work for our disobedience. Those who struggle to meet their needs feel it more keenly—they feel ashamed. But it is properly the shame that belongs to all of us. The author and poet Wendell Berry says:

> I believe...that the root of our racial problem in America is not racism. The root is our inordinate desire to be superior—not to some inferior or subject people, though this desire leads to the subjection of people—but to our condition. We wish to rise above the sweat and bother of taking care of anything—of ourselves, of each other, or of our country. We did not enslave African blacks because they were black, but because their labor promised to free us of the obligations of stewardship, and because they were unable to prevent us from enslaving them [1989, p. 112].

We stigmatize want and need. We also stigmatize "work that is fundamental and inescapable," to use Berry's phrase. This means ordinary human work—housekeeping, farming, maintenance and such. We glory in work that is optional to survival—in entertainment, higher education, trade in luxury items. To deny someone what is necessary to meet his needs, either materially or psychologically, is also deeply shaming.

In slavery the shaming of basic needs and of necessary work is as much a part of the transfer of shame as the beatings and the sexual abuse. In the slave system, the master is allowed to have needs and whims—the slave isn't. The slave exists solely to minister to the master's bidding. He is used as an object, valued solely for what he can do, and not for who he is. A slave society maintains the fiction that to have many needs and desires, and to have them all met by someone else, is a source of pride; while to have few needs and to meet them very modestly by oneself is a source of shame. People whose needs are routinely denied come to feel ashamed when they feel the needs arise. They come to feel ashamed of their needs as if the needs were the culprits. They may eventually come to disown their needs, and not to acknowledge them consciously, even to themselves (see Miller, 1997 & Bradshaw, 1988).

The scars of slavery

BECAUSE SLAVERY DID CREATE such a deep wound in our nation, let us examine more closely the scars that it has left in family life and society. What emotional habits would the slave system foster in the slaves, or indeed, in the owning class? The dominant race successfully transferred its feeling of original shame to the slaves. The slaves would react both by accepting the assessment that they were an inferior race, and by rebelling against it. The masters would feel pride in their ascendancy and power. The slaves would feel ashamed of their powerlessness, especially as family members were beaten and abused in front of one another.

They would suffer from slow-burning resentment, and hot-flashing anger. Anger, which could not be safely expressed against the masters, would sometimes be turned inward against self or against other slaves. Some would hear the Word of God imperfectly preached, and by grace, turn the energy of anger into powerful prayer—prayer for deliverance, prayer for their soul's salvation, and even prayer for their abusers.

What happens to this emotional legacy with emancipation? Is it just written off? The legacy of shame is unfortunately like an enormous, inherited debt—not easily written off or paid. Efforts are made through politics, business, and education, but little change is seen. Now over one hundred and fifty years later we perceive, not a steady march towards equal racial status, but cycles of progress and regression. Terror, rage, and hope are ever present and expressed in turn.

So, again, what does happen to this emotional legacy of shame with time? To follow one thread, the slave mothers found it dangerous to bond with their children and mates because they could and would be sold away at any time. They couldn't expect stable and supportive relationships with husbands. Slave women were valued as breeders, and only informal marriages were tolerated by the system. Deprived of protection and bred like animals, might they not feel resentment mixed with their maternal love?

Starting then and in subsequent generations, the emotionally deprived mother would perhaps feel resentful when her children clamored to have her meet their similar emotional needs. I mean the basic needs to be valued in and for themselves, the needs for love, bonding, affirmation of their feelings. She wonders: What makes them feel they're good enough to demand the things I did without? A child's cries for attention might get met with a sharp put-down, as the mother tried to put down the rising feelings from her own shamed childhood.

The stamp of the particular type of shaming experienced through slavery is still strongly imprinted on the African-American community. It has been passed from generation to generation, waiting to be recognized and addressed. There are scars of self-hatred shown by the desire to change hair texture and color, and other physical traits. There are the more obvious signs of addictions and violence. There are the scars of chronic abandonment of families by both fathers and mothers.

But the legacy of shame can be passed down in any family from any ethnic group; the pathways slash through ethnic and class categories. Generational shame can manifest through eating disorders, addictions, physical abuse, or abandonment—either physical or emotional. It can also manifest in a less obvious way through the quest for superior achievement. Over-achievement can also be driven by a desire to reduce the feeling of toxic shame.

Where psychology differs from the Church is that psychology still views shame as an issue involving this patient or that, this family or that. The Church teaches that it is at the core of the question of our fall and salvation. Salvation is precisely salvation from shame. I do not mean this in a reductionist way: *Eye hath not seen, nor ear heard, neither have entered into the heart of man, the things which God hath prepared for them that love him* (I Cor. 2:9). Apart from the liberation from shame, however, no one could receive or enjoy those superlative gifts.

FREEDOM IN CHRIST JESUS

Freedom from shame

I F THE SON THEREFORE *shall make you free, ye shall be free indeed* (Jn. 8:36). Jesus Christ has saved us from sin and death; He has freed us from the legacy of shame and made us joint-heirs with Him (cf. Rom. 8:17). Every commandment in the Bible, every counsel of the Holy Fathers is a liberation from shame. However, if an individual labors under a mountain of poisonous shame, it may be hard at first to take advantage of what Christ is freely offering when He says, *"Come unto Me all ye that labor and are heavy laden, and I will give you rest"* (Mt. 11:28). If our identity is based on toxic shame, "I am a mistake," rather than healthy shame, "I make mistakes," it can be hard to believe that Jesus loves us. The false identity begins to form long before we can think rationally.

The Church urges us towards saving humility, but when we try to say the penitential prayers in the services, or even the Jesus Prayer, we may feel that they shame us even more. We may want to edit out certain parts of the prayers—to omit phrases such as "sinners, of whom I am the first." Or we may agree with those sentiments in the wrong way. We may be saying in our heart, "mistakes, of which I am the first." Sinners are not mistakes. That is what the enemies of salvation want us to believe. Sinners are feverish children who, in their delirium, often project onto God the rejecting attitude that they have experienced from others.

How do we resolve unhealthy shame and learn to trust in Jesus' love? Of course this is a deeply personal and pastoral question for each one of us. Fortunately, He makes the first step for us toward healing. Nothing is more efficacious than the grace of the Holy Spirit, conferred by the Orthodox sacraments of Baptism and Chrismation. Since our original shame was the loss of the presence of the Holy Spirit in our hearts, then the Incarnation, Baptism, and Passion of our Lord and God and Saviour Jesus Christ are the remedy. We must pray that He will show us that all our worst sins are as a handful of dirt cast into the ocean of God's love. That our pain is from the wound of our common enemy, and not at all God's doing.

Healing work

IN OUR HEALING WORK, psychological techniques are useful if they help us to hold out our hand and to receive the grace which God already desires to bestow on us. The approach for each soul is unique. A good beginning is to realize that shame is an issue for everyone, because shame is the emotion that tells us all that we are all fallen. It helps to know that it is not only "me or my family or my racial group." We have to feel secure enough in supportive, therapeutic relationships for shame to begin to ease out from its hiding places. By therapeutic relationships, I don't necessarily mean formal counseling. Any relationship is potentially therapeutic where both parties try to live and love according to the Gospel. Where both parties try to be sensitive not to increase the other's unhealthy shame. Since we reject the parts of ourselves that we are ashamed of, and don't like to acknowledge that they are part of us, it helps considerably when a friend in Christ can see us for who we are and care about us. Whether or not that kind of love is available to us, we need to affirm our love and acceptance of the very parts that we don't like.

Many people with traumatic shame naturally try to push the bad feelings away. They hate the childlike side of themselves that gets panicky, and is easily triggered by anything that feels like abandonment or abuse. Some of them would feel great empathy for a real live child in front of them carrying the same pain and burden. But they often collude with their parents or society in blaming and shaming that inward, childlike part of their soul. If it's too daunting for people with traumatic shame to begin to approach the wounded part of the soul with loving curiosity, perhaps they can pray to our Lord Jesus for guidance in seeing and loving that part of self as He does. This is not the sin of self-love but quite the opposite.

The sin of self-love is really the sin of self-indulgence, of loving the sensual side of ourselves, and of ignoring the spiritual. God wants us to love ourselves correctly—that is, to work towards our salvation by following His commandments. To acknowledge that we are His handiwork and to treat ourselves with respect for His sake. Just as we love our friends and family members in spite of their physical and moral defects, we have to love ourselves. The issue here is not to get mixed up between faults and virtues, but rather to accept and embrace our whole self so that our whole self can come to Christ the Physician. Then the elements that are misdirected can be redirected (see Bradshaw, 1988). We can pray that the Lord Jesus will help us see that it is His presence in us that makes us worthy of love.

St. Paul said, *Be ye angry, and sin not* (Eph. 4:26a). It is better to love myself while still having a temper and getting angry than to be ashamed to acknowledge that I have the full range of human feelings. God created us all with the reactions of anger, fear, and sorrow. Anger or fear is elicited when we feel our wellbeing and safety are threatened. They are there to motivate us to protect ourselves. The problem is when we misunderstand the nature of the threat, because then our response is misdirected. Unacknowledged anger can seep out in a host of destructive ways—anything from a stubbornly uncooperative character to a major addiction. But if I love myself, appreciating my capacity for feeling anger, then I can ask God to help me redirect my anger from my neighbor, who certainly does not deserve the intensity of it, to the demons who most certainly do. My healthy shame will urge me to apologize for my slips and to be more prayerful and vigilant.

Forgiving our families

PERHAPS OUR PARENTS' emotional needs were poorly met, and they struggled imperfectly to meet ours. All people have had a fallen upbringing to some extent. It may seem as if we were there to meet our parents' emotional needs—to parent our parents—while no one was there for our needs. Or we may feel that we came from a model, loving family, but then why do we feel so messed up inside? In reality, all our family members have sinned against us and need our forgiveness. But how can we forgive if we don't acknowledge the hurts? Some people have to begin shame resolution by acknowledging their hurts. Young children blame themselves when they are hurt. They must deserve it, or their parents wouldn't hurt them. To admit that the parents are limited human beings who sin and err seems to breech a taboo. But to remember that our parents were sinned against by their parents, who were sinned against by their parents, all the way back to Eden, contextualizes our hurts. Our parents sinned against us, not because they were terrible people, but because they are fallen human beings, tempted by the evil one, just like everyone else.

Our parents and family members need our forgiveness, but not just the cheap forgiveness of saying, "It's not a big deal. Why remember the past? Live in the present." Real forgiveness requires acknowledging the hurts and grieving for the hurts. Grief resolves pain and loss. Grief involves retrieving pent-up, unconscious feelings and releasing them in a safe way—by writing them in a journal, crying on a strong shoulder, expressing them through a work of art. When the buried emotions are resolved, then we can tear up the grievance sheet against our family, and forgive them from the heart. We remember the past in order to set safe boundaries for ourselves, but we remember without rancor (see Stoop & Masteller, 1996). This step-by-step housecleaning of the cluttered rooms of our souls needs the guidance of an experienced and willing pastor or Christian psychotherapist, in the context of our ongoing sacramental life.

The memory of Paradise

WHEN WE GRIEVE for the imperfections of our upbringing—the imperfections of our family's expression of love for us—when we acknowledge that these things cause us deep pain, we are really grieving for the loss of Paradise. We are grieving for our fallen condition and the loss of our first estate. When our ancestral parents were cast out of Paradise, God settled them in a place nearby where they could constantly see it and remember the good from which they had fallen through disobedience (see Rose, 2000).

We make a great mistake when we idealize our family, our upbringing, and our past for the sake of supposed loyalty. We need to see the difference between how things truly are and how our heart longs for them to be. That longing is a remembrance of Paradise, which aids our salvation. That longing is intended to encourage us to seek fulfillment in God, and not to be satisfied with the things of this earth. The Lord said, *"Blessed are they that mourn, for they shall be comforted"* (Mt. 5:4).

We mourn for our sins, but we also mourn for the sins committed against us. We mourn for a paradisal childhood that was lost to us. But this redemptive mourning is with hope. For Christ also said that we must be born again, and become as little children in order to inherit the Kingdom of Heaven (see Mt. 18:2–3 & Jn. 3:3–8). A second birth is given to us through Baptism, and if a second birth, a second upbringing. The first upbringing by our families, in spite of their best intentions, is thrown off balance by the passions. The second upbringing is by the Holy Mother Church, directed by the Holy Spirit and aided by grace.

While psychologists say that we must mourn if we want healing from our shame, theirs is a mourning without existential hope—as those who mourn their dead without expecting the resurrection. While they would have us mourn the love we never experienced and the destruction of our souls in childhood, they only extend to us the hope of adjusting to the painful truth of the past and finding fulfillment in the present. But we Christians mourn with full hope that all of that for which we mourn will be fully restored and resurrected. Truly, through divine grace there is a resurrection of the soul, a restoration of the balance of heart, mind, and will, and a development of discernment between good and evil. In that state we are no longer tossed about like rudderless ships in a storm. St. Nikolai Velimirović describes this mature state of soul in his inimitable way:

> A true Christian is a mature man, ... who is distrustful of sensuality, who has a finer judgement and makes a finer distinction between the value of what is and what passes away. To the Christian, surely, clear guidance is given by the revelation of God to distinguish between good and evil; but he has need of long and serious study to reach perfection, to be able to know in every given situation what is good and what is evil. His knowledge must move inward to his feelings to be reliable and unmistaken. And both good and evil seek to touch the heart of man. It is therefore essential for a man to be practised in recognizing at once by the feeling of his heart what it is that ap-

proaches him, in just the same way as the tongue can immediately perceive the salt and the unsalted, the sweet and the sour [1985, p. 49].

The heart that is enveloped in shame is blinded by shame. It cannot distinguish good from evil. The heart that is liberated by Jesus Christ is free.

Summary

WE HAVE LOOKED AT SHAME as an emotion whether healthy or unhealthy. When it is healthy it leads to humility; when unhealthy, it leads to unbalance and to self-delusion, which is the first step of every sin. We have seen how toxic shame causes the formation of a false self—a cover-up, an aspect of what the Church calls the "old man." We have looked at shame as the reaction to our ancient banishment from God, and salvation as freedom from that shame. We have viewed it as a social phenomenon—both in the family and in society, especially through the phenomenon of slavery. We have also looked at shame as the unique, personal experience of the ancestral sin, and how its legacy is passed from generation to generation. Then again, we have explored how the feeling of shame gets transferred from one person or group to another through the projection of "shadow traits." And lastly, we have begun to look at the resolution of shame. That resolution entails fostering our healthy shame, and learning to recognize the symptoms of our unhealthy shame in our thoughts, our feelings, and our behavior. As we see it crop up in our lives, we shame shame by exposing it. We seek honesty with ourselves, with God, and in our relationships.

We still have disjointed parts of our make-up that war against themselves and God because of our fallenness and our unhealthy shame. As we walk the path of Christ, these parts will be balanced and healed, and discernment will begin to form. "His knowledge must move inward to his feelings to be reliable and unmistaken." This expresses the full healing of shame — the healing of shamed emotions and the flowering of humility. St. Nikolai finishes his earlier passage by telling us that when the mind, the heart, and the will become whole and reunited,

> when one is not dominant and the other subservient, then that man is filled with the peace that passes all understanding [Phil. 4:7], [that passes] all speech, all explanation, all fear and all sorrow. Then the small heaven within man begins to be like the great heaven of God, and the image and likeness of God then become clear within him [1985, p. 33].

Shame can truly be a master emotion holding us in the bonds of slavery. We want to *bind the strong man* (Mt. 12:29) concealed within us so that he will not bind our God-given capacity for love, for creativity, and for joy. It is for that reason that Jesus Christ our Liberator came down to earth. He was not afraid of mockery and rejection; nor was He afraid of deceit and treachery. For thirty pieces of silver, He was sold as a common slave. Hunted down by the law, He was crucified among common criminals. Having no guilt, He embraced shame and rejection so that we who are enslaved to sin need fear rejection no more.

Jesus is not afraid of our wounds; Jesus is not afraid of our needs; Jesus is not afraid of our sorrow. Let us come to Him with boldness and tell Him everything on our hearts. As we sacrifice our pain on the heart's altar, He will receive every offering as One Who has sweated His very Blood for us. He will free us from the legacy of shame and help us take on His easy yoke of humility. He will walk us step by step, as we can take those steps. From His overflowing goodness He will give us His courage, so that we may see ourselves with dispassion. From His overflowing kindness He will give us His love, so that we may see our neighbor with compassion.

From His overflowing wisdom He will give us His light, so that we may see God with the purified vision of our heart! To Him be glory and honor and victory and praise, together with His eternal Father and His life-giving Holy Spirit, now and forever. Amen.

References and Bibliography
First Essay

Berry, Wendell. (1989). *The hidden wound.* San Francisco: North Point.

Bradshaw, John. (1988). *Healing the shame that binds you.* Deerfield Beach, FL: Health Communications, Inc.

Cotton, Samuel. (1998). *The silent terror: A journey into contemporary African slavery.* New York: Harlem River.

Goleman, Daniel. (1987, September 15). "Shame steps out of hiding and into sharper focus." *The New York Times,* sec. 3, p. 1.

Mary, (Mother) & Ware, (Archimandrite) Kallistos, (Trans.). (1990). *The festal menaion.* South Canaan, PA: St. Tikhon's Seminary.

Matsakis, Aphrodite. (1998). *Trust after trauma: A guide to relationships for survivors and those who love them.* Oakland, CA: New Harbinger.

Miller, Alice. (1997). *The drama of the gifted child: The search for the true self.* (R. Ward, Trans.). New York: Basic Books.

Patterson, Orlando. (1982). *Slavery and social death: A comparative study.* Cambridge, MA: Harvard University.

——————. (1991). *Freedom,* vol. 1: *Freedom in the making of Western culture.* New York: Basic Books.

Rose, (Hieromonk) Seraphim. (2000). *Genesis, creation and early man: The Orthodox Christian vision.* Platina, CA: St. Herman of Alaska Brotherhood.

Solzhenitsyn, Aleksandr I. (1974). *The gulag archipelago, 1918—1956: An experiment in literary investigation,* I—II. (T. P. Whitney, Trans.). New York: Harper & Row.

Stoop, David & Masteller, James. (1996). *Forgiving our parents, forgiving ourselves: Healing adult children of dysfunctional families.* Ann Arbor, MI: Servant.

Theophan the Recluse, St. (1978). *Unseen warfare: The spiritual combat and path to Paradise of Lorenzo Scupoli edited by Nicodemus of the Holy Mountain and revised by Theophan the Recluse.* (E. Kadloubovsky & G. E. H. Palmer, Trans.). Crestwood, NY: St. Vladimir's Seminary.

Velimirović, St. Nikolai, (1985). *The prologue from Ochrid: Lives of the Saints and homilies for every day of the year,* vol. 1. (Mother Maria, Trans.). Birmingham, England: Lazarica.

Vitz, Paul C. (1994). *Psychology as religion: the cult of self-worship.* Grand Rapids, MI: Eerdmans & Carlisle, UK: Paternoster.

——————. (2005, March). "Psychology in recovery." *First Things.* Retrieved September 21, 2017 from https://www.firstthings.com/article/2005/03/psychology-in-recovery.

Wilson, Stanley D. (1991). *Rising above shame: Healing the family wounds to self-esteem.* Rockville, MD: Launch.

Second Essay, 2008:
Hope for Anger

Hope—a word that evokes images of the dawn, the birth of new life, and the tender new green of spring. And anger—thunder and lightning, storm and tempest and wave upon wave of destruction. And new hope in the rainbow—the promise that this raging destruction will never come again. There is one kind of hope in newness: the hope that potential will be fulfilled. There is another hope that dawns in the grip of destructive fury: the hope that the storm will pass, never to come again and, with that, the hope of healing.

In this essay we will follow the intricate dance between hope as mood, as attitude; and anger as emotion and also as attitude. Good hopes and bad hopes; good angers and bad angers—their dance that can lead equally to triumph or to shame. In this mix we will seek hope for the problem anger of individuals, of families, and between ethnic and racial groups. We will start by examining the meanings and range, first of hope, then of anger, and then the interplay.

We will want to weave in a biblical perspective, and so it is important to note from the outset that the word "hope" as we use it in today's English is basically equivalent to *elpis*, the word for "hope" in biblical Greek. *Elpis* is also translated as "trust." The ideas of hope, trust, and faith are closely interwoven. We tend to take it for granted that our English words and the original Greek basically mean the same thing, but with some words this is not the case, especially with the words that describe the experiences of anger — this we will deal with later.

CONCERNING HOPE

HOPE, TRUST, AND FAITH all have to do with confidence in a good future, with pleasant expectations, expectations of blessing or reward (see Louw, 1988). This is true if we think of the hope of spring — we look to the unfolding days ahead, we have expectations based on experience, expectations of relief from winter and the blessings of fair weather and the beauties of nature. This is also true if we think of the hope of the rainbow — we envision an end to the tempest, we wish ardently for this blessing, our expectations based partially on experience and partially just on the need to survive. Hope assesses prospects of success. In the ongoing project of living, we continually assess our expectations for success — both for our life as a whole and for particular undertakings. When we discover a basis for hope, this releases energy for us to make an effort.

Hope is both something we do and something we have; hope is a verb, or process, and hope is a noun, or entity. Hope, as a process, holds the key to our store of energy. A seed, for example, has energy locked inside: Hope is like the bringing together of warmth and moisture that unlocks the process of sprouting. In order for us to hope, we must bring together our thoughts about the future and our willingness to take a risk. Only then does hope release the energy for us to make a good effort. Hope has the built-in expectation that good actions will lead to good results.

Hope, as a noun, means the person, resources, strengths, or processes which form the basis of our good expectations. Hope, as a noun, also means the thing we hope for. The Scriptures teach us that hope is a virtue, but does this apply to every form of hope?

We place hope in the processes of nature when we hope for spring or wait for a birth. Again, we hope in a just cause and effect—good results for good causes and evil for evil causes. Thus we may place hope in the processes of negotiation and law, or in the processes of war. In a more personal dimension, we may place our hope in the rituals and celebrations of religion or, perhaps, in the processes of therapy.

Of course, we may locate our hope in a variety of entities as well. Science encourages us to place our hope in medicine and technology. Consumerism teaches us to hope in possessions. Our relational nature encourages us to place hope in family, social, and political groups. Impatience teaches us to place our hope in omens, portents, and dreams. Some of these are more dependable than others, but all can let us down.

We may also hope in ourselves—our talents, education, energy, or personality. We may have hope in our very will, or physical strength, aggression, or anger. In fact, without hope we do not feel angry at all; rather, we succumb to fear or paralysis, as we shall see further on in this discussion.

Of course, the only unfailing basis of hope is God Himself: "My hope is the Father; my refuge is the Son; my shelter is the Holy Spirit" (see UHB, 1997, pp. 235 & 253). Hope in God, His grace, and His promises releases the energy to live a virtuous life, to endure present storms in hope of heavenly reward.

The Scriptures teach plainly that trust in anything besides God is to be rejected although we do not reject the hope that God will work through nature and through people. Otherwise, why would we ordain clergy, bless oil and water, or offer bread and wine for God's transformation during the Sacrament? The question is not whether we trust in God to work through people, but whether we turn our backs on God to trust only in the human—whether it be ourselves, other people, medicine, technology, communications, negotiations, politics, and so on. *Thus saith the LORD: cursed be the man that trusteth in man, ... and whose heart departeth from the* LORD (Jer. 17:5). Departing from trust in God to trust only in what is human is a great source of anger and disappointment.

CONCERNING ANGER

WE MAY GAIN EASY ACCESS to the topic of anger through everyday experience, as it is more complex than hope to discuss from the Bible and the Fathers. The Church Fathers teach us that the passion of anger is in us, not in our circumstances, but looking at the circumstances is like looking at anger in a mirror. So we will begin by looking at the kinds of day-to-day situations that may elicit anger, be it self-protective, survival anger, or social anger. Next we will look at the various types of anger from a biblical point of view: This primarily entails social anger. Then we will examine the role of hope in the arousal of anger.

Typical anger situations

ANGER IS ELICITED by different types of situations: threats to wellbeing, unfair burdens, obstacles to pleasure and, finally, temptations to sin. Perceived threats to physical wellbeing trigger anger—either threats to ourselves or to a group or cause with which we identify. By group I mean family, school, church, ethnic group, nation, and so on. Thus anger against perceived physical threats results in interpersonal violence, legal actions, gang wars, riots, violence between races or ethnic groups, and international conflicts.

Likewise if we see a threat to our honor or that of our group or cause it may elicit our anger. Retaliation often comes in the form of maligning other people and groups with the intention, or at least the result, of damaging their name. Unfortunately, perceived threats to honor can elicit the same physical violence as threats to physical safety. The Church Fathers are quite forthcoming about this; we hear from St. Basil the Great:

Now what sorts of insults are exchanged? One calls the other a nobody and his mother and father, nobodies. The other calls the first a slave from slave parents. One says, "imbecile"; the other shouts, "maniac"; until, like ammunition, their insults are spent. Then, when their tongues run out of abuse, they move on to fist fighting. Thus, temper stirs up strife, strife turns to insults, insults lead to blows, blows to wounds, and from wounds, often enough, death results [see Basil, 1962, p. 451; Basil, 2005, p. 84].

St. Basil's words and insights are as fresh as if he were writing today. How many lives, then and now, have been wasted because of fights that began with insults?

We often target anger against the one we see meting out burdens or benefits unfairly. For example, someone who does not do their fair share of a common task, or a parent or supervisor who distributes jobs unevenly. Likewise the person who is quick to get recognition for other people's work or ideas may elicit our anger.

Obstacles to our physical ease or enjoyment come in various forms; these, too, may elicit our anger. For example, the obligation that comes on a day off, or the doctor or the diet that limits our favorite foods.

Finally, the best type of anger is against temptations to sin. This, the Fathers teach us, is why God gave us anger, so that by hating sin and temptation we might not fall into them.

Temper [*thumos*] is the sinew of the soul, which provides it with vigor for the accomplishment of good works. If the soul should become enervated from pleasure, anger hardens it as with a tincture of iron and restores it from a most weak and flaccid state to strictness and vigor. If your temper is not aroused against the Evil One, you will not be able to hate him as fiercely as he deserves. For I hold that it is necessary to have equal zeal for the love of virtue and the hatred of sin [see Basil, 1962, p. 456; Basil, 2005, p. 89].

May we always have a good supply of this kind of anger at hand. It is our best hope against sin. Now that we have examined the outer contexts of anger, let us look more closely at the phenomenon itself, both the experience of it and how we talk about it from the Bible—that is, how we understand biblical language compared with today's English.

The various dimensions of anger

IN ENGLISH, "ANGER" is an umbrella word that covers a range of meanings. We say "I'm angry" or "I'm mad" to convey feelings that range from mild annoyance to murderous rage. In biblical Greek, this is not so—There are two Greek words, *orgē* and *thumos*, that are commonly translated as "anger" or "wrath." These both denote manifest, high levels of agitation or malice, not mere annoyance or irritation.

Six dimensions of the anger experience are differentiated in the Scriptures and, likewise, in the Fathers of the Church. Two of these six dimensions pertain to non-problem anger, and four to problem anger. We'll go through this quickly just to orient to the big picture and then focus in on the aspects that are central to our topic. The first dimension of anger pertains to sorrow, distress, or regret that something happened. A person can say, for example, "I'm so mad that I got a traffic ticket today" without getting worked up, flushed, or punching a hole in the wall. The second pertains to indignation— the feeling that something is not right or fair and needs to be addressed. "It makes me so mad that in the 21st century there are still millions of enslaved people." While we may say "I'm angry" or "mad" in English, this is not what the Bible is talking about when it says to avoid anger.

The four types of problem anger are, first, the uncontrolled outburst of temper; second, vengefulness; third, bearing a grudge; and fourth, a quick temper and angry personality. The Fathers teach that anger comes to dominate a person's personality through practice and the force of habit. Anger is much easier to deal with before it becomes second nature. Since the first three types of problem anger cause the last, we will focus on the causative forms: the blow-up of temper, revenge seeking, and grudge bearing. These often define different stages of the same incident: for example, an outburst of temper is followed by a commitment to even the score, followed by a nagging feeling of resentment until revenge is taken.

There is a connection between anger and fear that we have not yet mentioned: Anger arousal and fear both begin with a sense of threat. Next comes hope in a process or action to get safe. If the greatest hope is to escape, then fear dominates anger; if the greatest hope is to stand our ground and fight, then anger dominates fear. If there is no hope of escape or victory, there is hope in slipping into a trance so as to endure the outcome with as little pain as possible.

Thus anger may be thought of as hope in aggression. As the energy is aroused for self-defense, our thinking quickly shifts gears. We move into a mode of extreme focus, pared-down logic, and quick assignment of blame. Under extreme threat, a nuanced sorting of cause and effect could cost life itself. Thus God has provided us with the ability to make snap judgments. Faced with a snarling dog, we quickly blame the dog for threatening us. Only on later reflection after the crisis do we blame the dog's owner or the lack of enforcement of leash laws. Likewise, the driver who cuts us off is instantly a "stupid idiot" regardless of his life accomplishments. We seldom reflect on whether we're at fault for speeding.

This simplified logic works well against snarling dogs and we get by with it in traffic, but it does not work as well in social situations which are often very complex. We are still inclined to make snap judgments and, if our initial efforts at self-defense are thwarted, we may bear a grudge and plot revenge.

HEALING ANGER

Remedies for anger

THE FATHERS OF THE CHURCH reflected quite a bit on anger: Most of the writers were monks and bishops. They tended to write either for other men living in male communities, or to write Sunday sermons for lay congregations. Their writings often assumed that the hearer or reader was another adult male, living in a context where life-threat from within his community was rare, and where most anger provocations came as threats to his physical comfort or his honor. The remedy they gave for the first was to war against the love of physical pleasure; the remedy for the second was humility.

These writers also gave very specific advice for the different types of anger. The Holy Orthodox Church teaches the same wisdom now as in the early centuries, offering hope against the temper outburst, hope against vengefulness, and hope against grudge-bearing. I find it particularly hopeful that present-day psychology is rediscovering many of the things the ancient Church taught. Truly God is not stingy with His truth, but rewards all earnest seekers.

The Church offers this hope against fury or temper: "When we are angry we should remain silent. Then we must immediately ask for God's mercy and assistance so that we can get rid of our anger" (Markides, 2005, p. 72). Orthodox writers describe this as "choking the anger" (cf. p. 71). In this action we are actually redirecting and harnessing the energy of anger into a powerful prayer, just as we harness the raw energies of nature with windmills and hydroelectric stations. The result is that after trying this several times, our temper becomes milder.

Today's psychology complements this teaching, advising people to do the opposite of what the anger impulse demands: Instead of raising the voice, to speak softly; instead of glaring, to smile; instead of leaning forward or looming, to sit back. Some therapists advise people to sign a written resolution not to let their temper explode for 24 hours, no matter what happens, and to invite someone to hold them responsible to this. After initial success, they progress to longer periods (see McKay & Rogers, 2000). People also learn to take a time out for their anger during which they harness their energy for useful physical ends.

Then and now, people have learned to think differently about their anger provocations. The Fathers ask: If a person says something true about us, why get angry? If it is untrue, why not despise it rather than lashing back? They bring examples from Scriptures of how holy men of old dealt with taunts and name-calling.

Today's psychology also offers hope for anger through new ways of thinking. People are taught to notice how often they raise their wishes to laws that others "should" obey. "I shouldn't have to be the one to go to him; he should know he offended me. He should be the one to call me!" How often do we say that sort of thing? The truth is I would *rather* not be the one to make the first move. I *wish* the other person would know I was hurt and care enough to call. Anger management may not use the word "humility," but it tries to foster it just the same.

The Bible teaches us not to condemn a person's character because of some wrongdoing. It is better to say: "The child stole a candy" than to say: "The child is a thief." Anger management also teaches us not to apply destructive labels to people (see Weisinger, 1985).

In addition, anger management teaches us not to act like mind readers— "She did that on purpose, just to vex me!" How do you know? (see Weisinger, 1985). We tend to get much angrier about intentional hurts than accidental ones. Perversely, anger becomes an inventor of intentions.

According to St. John Climacus there is a progression by which temper or fury is tamed:

> First there is a forced silence of the lips while the mind and emotions are seething; next the mind is free of blaming and condemning thoughts while the emotions are stirred; and finally there is an inner mastery over thoughts and feelings [JCL, 8:4, p. 81; PG 88:828. As translated by Weston, 2008a, p. 8].

Hope for vengefulness comes a bit differently. It comes primarily from trusting in God's providence and justice, and embracing humility. Pertaining to trust in divine providence, St. Abba Dorotheos says:

> When we hear something, we immediately react like a dog who when somebody throws a stone forgets the person who threw it and runs after the stone to bite it. That is how we react. We abandon God who permits opportunities to purify ourselves from our sins and we run to our neighbor saying, "Why did you speak to me like that? Why did you do this to me?" [ADP, 2000, p. 149].

Pertaining to trust in God's justice, the Epistle to Hebrews says *Vengeance belongs to me; I will pay them back* (10:30). While the Lord's parable of the widow and the unjust judge (Lk. 18:1–8a) is primarily about persistence in prayer, it also teaches us to leave vengeance to God. As you remember, the widow comes to the unjust judge daily saying *Grant me justice against my opponent!* The unjust judge eventually resolves to help her just to be rid of her. The parable concludes: *Won't God grant his chosen people justice when they cry out to him day and night? Is he slow to help them? I tell you, he will give them justice quickly.* The Lord teaches us to persevere in prayer against our enemy—anger—and that He will vindicate us. He also teaches us to leave justice in His hands, and not to avenge ourselves against our earthly enemies. It takes humility to cry out for help, because we must acknowledge our own limitations. (A first principle of 12-step programs, by the way.) It takes humility to be patient with insults and humiliations. But it also helps to think that we perhaps suffer for hidden sins.

The remedies for vengefulness also apply to resentment with the addition of certain instruction in prayer. According to St. Maximos the Confessor, hope against grudge-bearing and resentment comes from prayer for the offender (III *Love*, v. 13; PCT 2: 84–85). St. Dorotheos encourages us to go a step further and to pray to be saved by the prayers of the one who offended us (ADP, 2000, p. 157).

Ancient wisdom, present struggles

LET US REFLECT AGAIN on the early Church authors: as we observed above, they were mostly writing for male audiences; they were also writing for men who were born into an honor-based society. We still have honor-based subgroups in our society where persons—male and sometimes female—are expected to retaliate physically for an insult. If they fail to then they are considered weaklings and cowards, and they are in danger of assault from other group members. It was to people of an honor-based society that Jesus Himself first preached turning the other cheek and walking the extra mile (see Mt. 5:39 & 41). This initial preaching of humility was indeed radical; it is therefore no wonder that the Monastic Fathers spent so much time elaborating this theme of humility, so necessary if men are to live together peacefully with each other and with their wives and families.

There are some contexts of anger and violence today that were not fully anticipated by the early Church writers. This does not mean that their texts are irrelevant to contemporary issues. Rather we may have to search more diligently for appropriate ones.

Family violence seems to be one of these areas and ethnic conflict another. James Poling, in Protestant context, offers a thought-provoking treatment of these issues. Dealing with family violence, in his experience, is completely taboo in the Church. He faults the Church for not preaching against this form of sin:

> Violent men have a right to ask the church: *How could I be violent toward someone I love? How could the church allow me to engage in this behavior to the damnation of my soul and not confront me with God's judgment and grace?* Most men who have come to me for help are at a total loss to face these questions themselves. They have never heard sermons, Bible studies, prayers, or spiritual guidance on these issues [2003, p. 32].

Poling goes on to make this further observation about his own limitations as a pastor:

> In order to talk about child abuse in the church, I must be able to talk about my own potential for abuse. But how can a Christian confess an act of child abuse? The church has its list of approved sins—using profanity, not going to church enough, watching a questionable movie. But confessing child abuse? I had never heard a Christian talk this way, and I wasn't volunteering to be the first [2003, p. 37].

Poling's experience of Church never prepared him to deal with these issues. Indeed, in the Early Church, the model of family conflict was unbelievers (or weak believers) persecuting believers. *Do not think that I came to bring peace on earth. I did not come to bring peace but a sword. ... A person's enemies will be members of his own family* (Mt. 10:34 & 36).

This enmity included mothers begging their children to deny Christ so as to preserve their lives. It included pagan fathers pursuing believing daughters to demand sexual favors of them. It included pagan fathers killing daughters who refused pagan suitors.

However St. John Chrysostom, at least, was aware of family violence among Christians and did not shrink from preaching and teaching against it. St. Basil the Great proved himself a great anthropologist in describing the raging man whose face becomes unrecognizable, his words incoherent and whose "hands are lifted even against his kinsfolk [while] all the limbs of his body attack. His feet trample ruthlessly upon the most vital organs and everything at hand becomes a weapon for his fury" (Basil, 1962, pp. 449–450; 2005, p. 83).

The following texts all assume the man is potentially violent toward his wife and, perhaps, his children. I know from my clinical work that family violence can and does happen in all possible configurations: not only males against females, but males against males, females against males, and females against females; the older against the younger and the younger against the older. The Church Fathers may not expound on every possible situation, but they do say enough for us to bring light to the various contexts of family violence that we find today.

The Epistle writers placed household codes of conduct in various letters. St. Peter sets forth the duties of husbands saying: *You husbands must live with your wives in an understanding manner, as with the weaker, feminine body. Honor them as heirs with you of the gift of life, so that nothing may interfere with your prayers* (1 Pet. 3:7). Hilary of Arles comments on this verse: "Men must accept that they are stronger than their wives and therefore have a duty to protect them" (ACC, vol. 11, p. 100). Severus of Antioch adds that "nothing so hinders the work of God like trouble in the home" (ACC, vol. 11, p. 99).

St. Paul likewise includes codes of conduct in Ephesians 5 and Colossians 3. In Ephesians he describes the union of man and wife as like that of Christ and the Church. St. Chrysostom waxes eloquent here:

> Take then the same provident care for her as Christ takes for the Church. Yes, even if it should be needful for you to give your life for her ... and to undergo any suffering whatever, do not refuse it.

He then proceeds to teach the husband how to treat his wife when the threat to their peaceful coexistence comes, not from without, but from her:

> Even if you see her looking down on you, and disdaining and scorning you, yet by your great thoughtfulness for her, by affection, by kindness will you be able to win her over [NPNF, 1, 13: 144].

What he implies here, he makes more explicit when commenting on Colossians: St. Chrysostom interprets the passage *Husbands, love your wives, and be not bitter against them* (Col. 3:19) to mean they should not fight with them (NPNF, 1, 13: 304).

In his Homily 26 on I Corinthians he adds that a man must not allow himself to strike his wife for any cause—he should not even strike the maid, let alone his wife. He advances his argument from various directions, shaming the Christian man into behaving better than the pagan: Even pagan laws permitted a woman to leave the husband who struck her. Then he exaggerates to drive his point home: If you can even call the batterer a man rather than a beast, it is one and the same as if this man had killed his own mother. At God's command he left his father and mother to take a wife (see Gen. 2:24) and now beats the wife for whose sake he left his mother. Finally he appeals to the manly sense of honor, saying that sometimes

> shrieks and wailings are borne along the alleys, and there is a running to the house of him that is so disgracing himself, both of the neighbors and the passers by, as though some wild beast were ravaging within.

Such a man should rather be buried alive than to show himself in public afterward (NPNF, 1, 12:156).

After looking at how men should treat their wives, it is appropriate to look at the verses in Ephesians and Colossians concerning parents and children—*Fathers, do not provoke your children lest they become discouraged* (Col. 3:21) and, *Fathers, do not provoke your children to wrath, but bring them up in the nurture and admonition of the Lord* (Eph. 6:4). Commentaries on these similar passages give examples of how the injunction not to anger one's children applies both when they are young and when they are older. For young children it is important to set a good example of biblical behavior and to teach them from Scripture. Then, as now, children were inundated with worldly messages from the culture and amoral "superheroes." Then they were from mythology; now from film.

Contemporaries John Chrysostom and Ambrose of Milan both reflect on the importance of treating children fairly. Examples include treating them as free children and not slaves and also being fair with their inheritance. Some fathers slight the children of a former marriage and favor the children of the current wife. Parents need to be good examples of undiscriminating love to their children (see ACC vol. 8, 1999 & vol. 9, 2000).

Psychotherapy bears out St. Paul's insight: When children are angered by the injustice of a parent they love, it is deeply confusing and thus demoralizing. It affects children, not only on a personal level and on the level of ethical development, but even on a neurological level. When a young person's nervous system can't decide whether to approach the parent in love, rise up against him in anger, or flee from him in fear, the unsolvable dilemma disorganizes the development of important neurological circuits.

Regarding the behavior of spouses and parents, we see that some family violence erupts in the heat of the moment — manifested in words, yelling, and threatening actions. But other times it is a matter of coolly eliciting anger in others — wounding them by injustice and hypocrisy.

Why have I presented so many scriptural verses and ancient commentaries on family harmony and violence? In part because I find all around me such a concern for decent appearances. Much family violence happens covertly, perpetrated by men and women who do all they can to keep up appearances, who attend church regularly, or even have leadership roles there. The ones with the power to be violent say by word or attitude: "My violence is not the problem, but if you tell the family secret that is what will bring us all to ruin." The victim who finally tells about the violence is blamed by all for wrecking the family and the financial security and causing legal entanglements. It is not the violent person's fault at all. These families have learned to place their hope on the shakiest possible ground: They place their hope on secrecy and silence. They do this as if to say, "There is no real hope for change, for peace and harmony, but if we all keep a compact of silence, we will enjoy respect and honor in society."

The true teaching of the Church, that God can and does bring good from evil circumstances, may become subtly perverted. Both perpetrators and victims come to believe that God somehow needed the evil to happen in order to bring about good. For example, some children remain silent about abuse, continuing to receive food, shelter, clothing, and education. Then they may come to feel that they somehow wanted the abuse because that was the only way for them to have their needs met. God doesn't need anyone to be abused to meet their needs. God can work things out from any starting point. He is never complicit in the abuse and He does not need it in order to provide for His children.

Guidance for wives and children

WHAT BIBLICAL PRECEPT should wives follow to deal with their husbands' excessive anger—is it submit to your husbands (cf. Eph. 5:22 & Col. 3:18) or turn the other cheek (cf. Mt. 5:39) or when they persecute you in one place, run to another? (cf. Mt. 10:23). An important, but easy-to-overlook point is that both wives and children are enjoined to submit to the head of the household *in the Lord* (Col. 3:18 & Eph. 6:1). This "in the Lord" means that it is not an absolute or servile obedience, but a submission that keeps the Lord and His precepts first. If the man directs something that is not in the Lord, then wives and children must follow their conscience (cf. NPNF, 1, 13:153 & 304).

It is important to protect children, not only from being targets of violence, but also from observing it. Our growing understanding of trauma suggests that helplessly witnessing abuse to another can, at times, be more damaging than being the direct target of abuse (ISPT, May 12, 2008). Thus for children to witness parental fights, whether by seeing or by overhearing, can be very traumatic for them; it can affect their capacity to form loving relationships as adults. As an aside, in the days of legalized slavery in the US, it was a common practice to whip one family member while compelling others to watch helplessly. The sense of being totally powerless to help a loved one can profoundly change a person's sense of self.

The difficulties parishes have in dealing with family violence know no denominational boundaries: A woman from an Orthodox parish finally made a CPS (Children's Protective Services) report against her husband—he was violent toward their children and she knew it was her duty to protect them. She did this reluctantly after several attempts at pastoral intervention had failed. Instead of offering their support, other members of the church began to shun her for making their problems public. Especially other women who had endured abuse in silence felt it was this woman's duty to do the same. The result is that the woman who spoke up to protect her children from violence is banned from going to church, not the violent perpetrator.

But I applaud this woman for speaking the truth, and perhaps opening the door for other families to get help. This provides hope for the future generations that violence does not have to be blindly accepted as a way of life. The ancient Christians understood the Church as a hospital for sinners, not as a club for the righteous. There is no reason for a parish to have undue shame if it comes out that members have domestic problems. Does not the Lord say the same? *I did not come to call righteous people, but sinners* (Mt. 9:13b).

Hope for toxic feelings

UNLIKE FAMILY VIOLENCE, ethnic (or racial) conflict is not decried in the ancient writings. Early Church literature is full of conflict between Orthodox believers and pagans, Jews and, after the 6th century, the children of Hagar—that is Muslims. But the unfortunate situation that we face in our time, that people of the same faith should fight because of the color of their skin was not envisioned by the 4th to 7th century writers.

In the ancient world stereotyping people groups was considered normal and everyone did it—they even did it to themselves. St. Paul reports: One of their very own prophets said, *"Liars ever, men of Crete, Savage brutes that live to eat"* (Tit. 1:12). The conclusion that he draws from this rather vicious stereotype, however, is not that Cretans should be beaten, enslaved, and tormented. The lesson, rather, is that Titus should refute them sharply so that they may become healthy in the faith (see Tit. 1:13b).

In the case of family violence, the Church's tradition of care for the weak and the defenseless should set the tone. In the case of ethnic and racial hostility, St. Paul's teaching is that in Christ *there is neither Jew nor Greek, there is neither bond nor free, there is neither male nor female: for ye are all one in Christ Jesus* (Gal. 3:28). The principles of unity and care for the weak are clear, but how do we get there from where we are as a society? I spoke first of the need to address family violence because I believe strongly that this is the key to dealing with social violence.

One of the greatest perpetrators of ethnic and racial violence in recent memory was Adolph Hitler. In Adolph's childhood, his father, Alois Hitler, beat his mother and older half-brother until the latter left home. The father, a heavy drinker, came to beat Adolph daily.

As a man, Hitler reminisced: One day, after reading in his favorite adventure author that

> "the brave man gives no sign of being in pain, I made up my mind not to let out any sound next time I was beaten. And when the moment came I counted every blow. My mother thought I'd gone mad when I proudly told her, 'Father hit me thirty-two times'" [Lambert, 2008, p. 61].

Meanwhile, his doting mother tried to make it up to him. Young Adolph and his mother shared camaraderie in their fear of Alois Hitler. I would expect that as a young boy, watching his beloved mother get beaten and being unable to help her would have produced powerful feelings of shame. Later when he started getting his own beatings, the same would have been reinforced, until the triumphant day when he learned to be proud of his toughness.

Controversial author Alice Miller reflected on how these early experiences formed the Führer and I believe that her empathetic reading of him is on point.

> It was in this way—through total denial of his pain, his feelings of powerlessness and desperation; that is, through the denial of the truth—that Hitler fashioned himself into the master of violence and inhuman cynicism that he became. The result was a primitive human being incapable of empathy for other human beings [Miller, 1997, p. 85].

We can only wonder what would have allowed Hitler and his followers to wake up, to feel and mourn their pain, and realize

> that the people who cheated them, who engendered their misery, their hunger for power and destruction were not Jews or Turks or Arabs or Gypsies, but their very own parents—clean, orderly citizens, God-fearing respectable churchgoers [Miller, 1997, p. 84].

I have focused on Hitler because of his program of ethnic and racial "cleansing"; Stalin from Russia, however, and Romania's Ceausescu also grew up as abused children. Alice Miller believes that they all heard childhood messages that they were being harshly disciplined "for their own good." Just as their parents professed to "save" them through violence, these men, as dictators, professed to "save" their nations through violence, with devastating results (Miller, 1997).

It is said that in wars from Vietnam to recent ones, a disproportionate number of those who volunteer have survived traumatic childhoods. It is almost as if the childhood desire to master the situation in which they were powerless and afraid drives them in adulthood to become "army strong," seeking out violent, dangerous situations in their new, powerful role. I wonder what we would discover if we could learn the backgrounds of the people who have perpetrated racial violence in this country from the earliest times until now.

Let me make this important distinction: While it is often the case that angry or violent people were abused, it does not follow that most abused people become perpetrators of abuse or violence. Quite the contrary, a large number are anxious not to hurt others as they have been hurt. I find this very hopeful.

To the degree that, with God's help, we restore the peace of the Holy Spirit in our marriages and families, perhaps the social and racial violence will begin to take care of itself. Our children will grow up in the conscious hope of fulfilling their potential in the context of godly relationships, as integral members of the body of Christ.

In conclusion

THERE IS HOPE FOR ANGER in anger. I believe that many violent people cannot imagine life being different, especially if their own childhoods were violent. If they glimpse, through the lives of others, that things could have been different, they will be furious at the deception that blinded them. And they will begin that blessed mourning which is rewarded by the Comforter. When they learn to feel, to name, and tolerate their own feelings there is hope for their anger. There is hope for anger in naming it "anger"; in saying "I feel furious" rather than "I feel like hitting someone."

There is hope for anger in knowing that the Orthodox Church has a long history of facing and telling the truth about human passions and relationships. The Church Fathers not only exhort families to live in love and harmony, they also tell, step by step, how men and women can overcome their tempers, their vengefulness, their grudge-bearing and, through this, their angry personalities.

There is hope in remembering that interpersonal aggression is a sign of misplaced hope—a better, higher hope must be offered before hope in violence will be relinquished. This better hope must be demonstrated in order to be shared. Our Savior endured the aggression of others without retaliating or being destroyed. In Him we must learn to do the same. This is the hope of the rainbow after the tempest. This is the hope of the Resurrection of the soul in and through our Lord and God and Savior Jesus Christ, to Whom be the honor and the glory and the victory and the majesty. Amen.

List of Abbreviations

ACC—see Oden, Thomas C., (Gen. Ed.), *Ancient Christian commentary on Scripture. New Testament.*

ADP—see Dorotheos, St. (Abba).

ISPT—Indiana Society for Psychoanalytic Thought. (Unpublished discussion.)

JCL—see John Climacus, St.

NPNF—see Schaff, Philip, (Ed.), *A select library of the Nicene and Post-nicene Fathers of the Christian Church.*

PCT—see Palmer, G. E. H., et al., *The philokalia: The complete text.*

PG—see Migne, J.-P., (Ed.), *Patrologiæ cursus completus. Series Græca.*

UHB—see Holy Trinity Monastery, *The unabbreviated horologion or book of the hours.*

References and Bibliography
Second Essay

Basil the Great, St. (4th cent/1962). *The Fathers of the Church: A new translation,* vol. 9, (R. J. Deferrari, Ed.); *St. Basil: Ascetical works,* (Sr. M. M. Wagner, Trans.). Washington, DC: The Catholic University of America Press.

——————. (4ᵗʰ cent/2005). *On the human condition,* (Nun N. V. Harrison, Trans. and Ed.). Crestwood, NY: St. Vladimir Seminary.

Dorotheos, St. (Abba). (6ᵗʰ cent/2000). *Abba Dorotheos, practical teaching on the Christian life,* (C. Scouteris, Trans. & Ed.). Athens: Epimelia S.A., Greek Advertising Co.

Holy Trinity Monastery. (1997). "The prayer of St. Joannicius." In *The unabbreviated horologion or book of the hours.* Jordanville, NY: Holy Trinity Monastery.

John Chrysostom, St. (4ᵗʰ cent/1979). *Homilies on the epistles of Paul to the Ephesians.* In Schaff, P. (Ed.). (1800s/1979). *A select library of the Nicene and Post-nicene Fathers of the Christian Church,* vol. 12. Grand Rapids, MI: Wm. B. Eerdmans.

John Climacus, St. (c. 649/1991). *The ladder of divine ascent,* revised ed., (A. L. Moore and Holy Transfiguration Monastery, Trans.). Brookline, MA: Holy Transfiguration Monastery.

Lambert, Angela. (2008). *The lost life of Eva Braun.* New York: St. Martin's.

Louw, J. P., Nida, E. A., Smith, R. B. & Munson, K. A. (1988). *Greek-English lexicon of the New Testament based on semantic domains,* vol. 1. New York: United Bible Societies.

Markides, Kyriacos C. (2005). *Gifts of the desert: The forgotten path of Christian spirituality.* New York: Doubleday.

McKay, Matthew & Rogers, Peter. (2000). *The anger control workbook.* Oakland, CA: New Harbinger.

Migne, J.-P. (Ed.). (1860–1885). *Patrologiæ Græcæ,* vols. 23, 31, 55, 82, 88, 90, 123, 125. Paris: Migne.

Miller, Alice. (1997). *Breaking down the wall of silence: The liberating experience of facing painful truth.* New York: Meridian.

Oden, Thomas C. (Gen. Ed.). (1999). *Ancient Christian commentary on Scripture. New Testament,* vol. 8, (M. Edwards, Ed.). Downers Grove, IL: InterVarsity.

——————. (Gen. Ed.). (2000). *Ancient Christian commentary on Scripture. New Testament,* vol. 9, (P. Gorday, Ed.). Downers Grove, IL: InterVarsity.

——————. (Gen. Ed.). (2008). *Ancient Christian commentary on Scripture. New Testament,* vol. 11, (G. Bray, Ed.). Downers Grove, IL: InterVarsity.

Palmer, G. E. H., Sherrard, P. & Ware, K. (Trans. and Eds.). (1979 – 1995). *The philokalia: The complete text,* vols. 1 – 4. London: Faber and Faber.

Poling, James N. (2003). *Understanding male violence: Pastoral care issues.* St. Louis, MO: Chalice.

Reitz, Ronda R. (1999). Batterers' experiences of being violent: A phenomenological study. *Psychology of Women Quarterly.* 12, 143 – 165.

Schaff, Philip (Ed.). (1800s/1979). *A select library of the Nicene and Post -nicene Fathers of the Christian Church,* vols. 12 & 13. St. Chrysostom: *Homilies on the epistles of Paul.* Grand Rapids, MI: Wm. B. Eerdmans.

Velimirović, St. Nikolai. (1986). *The prologue from Ochrid: Lives of the Saints and homilies for every day of the year,* vol. 2, (M. Maria, Trans.). Birmingham: Lazarica.

Weisinger, Hendrie. (1985). *Dr. Weisinger's anger work-out book.* New York: Harper.

Weston, (Nun) Katherine. (2008). *Anger: Integrating psychotherapy with Eastern Orthodox anthropology.* A presentation for the Third International Conference of Orthodox Psychotherapists, Sarasota, FL, January 2 – 5.

Third Essay, 2007:
Forgiving the Prodigal

If the whole of Holy Scripture of the New Testament
were lost, and only this story preserved, ...
it would deliver to us in a nutshell
the entire evangelical teaching, that is, what is sin,
what is true repentance, what straightening
one's life means, and what is salvation.
— *Patriarch Pavle, 1996*

I REMEMBER A ROAD TRIP, now well over a decade ago. A certain Fr. Gerasimos was driving and I was in the passenger seat with his older son—my godson—cozy between us. Father began to tell us a story about a nun, a little boy and their adventures in the woods. It wasn't about me; it was about Mother Katrina. And the boy was not Marty, but very much like him. Father kept us spellbound mile after mile. There is something so intimate and engaging about being written into a story. There is something about having a character like us, but not quite, that opens us up to see our problems and our possibilities from a fresh vantage point.

A parable is all that and more, because it teaches a lesson; it rebukes, it warns, it encourages, it gives hope. When King David committed adultery and murder—killing his soldier Uriah the Hittite with the sword of their enemy and taking his wife for his own—Nathan the prophet convicted him with a parable. At first, David heard the parable as a true-life story about another man—a merciless rich man who coveted and stole the one comfort a certain poor man had. He became furious and

61

swore that the man should die and restore the poor man's possession four-fold. Then Nathan told David, *You are that man* (II Sam. 12:7). David turned his anger against his own sin. He wrote the most beautiful psalm of repentance: *Have mercy on me, O God, according to Thy great mercy; and according to the multitude of Thy compassions blot out my transgression* (Psa. 50:1). David saw himself and repented.

And both the Pharisees and the scribes grumbled saying, "This man receives sinners and eats with them!" (Lk. 15:2). Now these scribes, also known as sages, were the scholars and experts in interpreting the law of Moses. Pharisee, *Perushim* in Hebrew, means "separated." Those of the Pharisaic sect were "set apart," "separated" from others as "organized followers" of the Jewish sages, to conform their lives exactingly to the precepts of the Torah (Danker, 2000, p. 1049). According to some scholars, at the time of Jesus the Pharisees numbered about 6,000. "They formed a closely knit order into which one had to be initiated and from which one could be expelled for nonconformity" (Douglas, 1974, p. 772).

The Lord Jesus, in his compassionate desire to correct and heal, characterized the Jewish sages and Pharisees in different parables. Luke first sets forth the parable of the lost sheep and the ninety-nine who did not stray (15:3–7). The sages and their disciples, as a group, are the ninety-nine; the sinner is the one that is lost. Then he relates the parable of the lost coin (15:8–10). Then, he records, the Lord elaborated further by telling the parable of the lost son. We will examine the last portion, dealing with the older brother, from many angles. Although it's familiar, I encourage you to read it afresh; I translated this portion from the Greek for our reflection:

> But his son—the older one—was out on the farm and as he came and drew near the house he heard the music and dancing. Then after calling aside one of the servants he asked what these things

might mean. And the servant told him: "Your brother is here, and your father has killed the calf—the grain-fed one—because he received him safe and sound." But the son was furious and didn't want to go in; however his father went out and pleaded with him. But he answered his father saying, "Look—all these years I have been serving you and never once broke your rules, and you never gave me a kid so that I could have a good time with my friends. But now this son of yours who squandered all your wealth on prostitutes comes and for him you killed the grain-fed calf!" Then he said to him, "Child, you are always with me, and all that is mine is yours. It was right to rejoice and celebrate because this brother of yours was dead and has come to life; he was lost and is found [Lk. 15:25–32; author's translation].

Most discussions of this parable focus on the Prodigal as an icon of repentance and on the father as an image of our heavenly Father. But who really is the most important character? I suggest that from a certain perspective it is the older son, because it was in this figure that the Lord cast the Jewish sages and their disciples in the parable, just as Nathan the prophet characterized King David in his parable about the covetous rich man. It is for the sake of the sages and Pharisees, cast as the older son, that the whole drama unfolds.

The parable was spoken for the benefit of those who *trusted in themselves that they were righteous, and despised others* (Lk. 18:9b) and whose sense of justice was affronted by God's mercy toward sinners (see Bl. Theophylact, pp. 202–203). The Pharisees as a group are characterized as resenting and resisting the rehabilitation of the most despised elements of society. The older son represents the Pharisees and, not only the Pharisees, but all who trust that they are righteous; while the younger son represents all evil-doers and transgressors. Just as the Lord rebuked David for having the outward form of righteousness but lacking compassion for his fellow man, so He rebukes the Jewish sages and Pharisees for having the outward form of righteousness, but lacking the one thing needful—love.

When we understand the older brother properly as a characterization of the Pharisaic sect, we can round out his portrayal using other references and parables from the Lord. Here the Lord brings to light the inward disdain of the "separated ones," the Pharisees, toward sinners: *The Pharisee stood and prayed thus in himself, O God, I thank You that I am not like other men, extortioners, unjust, adulterers, or even like this publican* (Lk. 18:11). The prayer of the older son might be revised to say "Thank God I am not like other people—thieves, crooks, immoral, or even like this so-called brother of mine."

This is not to say that all Pharisees thought this way, because some were found among the Lord's followers—some like Nicodemus and later the Apostle Paul. But separating from others to prove themselves better—better obviously, for who would separate to prove themselves worse—was the purpose of the Pharisaic sect. In the Gospels this is portrayed as part of their group identity. To be a member in good standing, this is how one had to present himself. In this sense, the parable is not only telling us something about how we behave as individuals—how we all have a bit of the older son in us—but also how we human beings behave in groups. This is where I would like us now to turn our attention. At this point we will set aside the parable for a bit in order to look at groups from different angles.

The complexities of group life

THOSE WHO MAKE A STUDY of how we humans behave in groups all agree that it is much more complex than studying the behavior, attitudes, and spiritual dispositions of one person. Here are a few things that come to mind that make for that complexity. We are not designed by God to be complete in ourselves. For an obvious example, no one can produce a child on their own. We need one another so that in community all the necessary attributes and abilities will be present.

Also, we human beings have a deep internal connection at the level of being. We are connected mystically with everyone else. As Elder Porphyrios says,

> Man is a mystery. We carry within us an age-old inheritance— all the good and precious experience of the prophets, the saints, the martyrs, the apostles and above all of our Lord Jesus Christ; but we also carry within us the inheritance of the evil that exists in the world from Adam until the present [SHCC, 2005, p. 134].

More particularly, "Every person has incorporated into himself the experiences of his parents and especially of his mother" (p. 174). This marks some people more deeply than others, and the effects obviously may be positive or negative. Thus in any given group, not only are the members present, but so is what they have internalized of their parents, grandparents, and the good and evil of this world. At any given time in a group context we respond, not just to the person in front of us, but to their internalized others. Or we respond in a certain way because they remind us of someone we knew before—perhaps someone in our own family.

If, in reading these layers of complexity, you feel a bit overwhelmed, that is how people generally feel about the complexities of group life. In fact, one of the first things we people do in groups is try to simplify how we understand our social world. One way we do this is by seeing issues and people's positions on them as more black-and-white than they really need to be. Some people are idealized as better than they really are while others are seen as hopelessly bad. Another way we do this is by assigning roles. There are many dyadic roles of giving and receiving such as therapist-client, teacher-student, author-reader. In this class of dyads, the giving is expected to be mostly one-way. This is not because the client, student, or reader is any less gifted or intelligent; the "one-way" assumption simplifies the social contract and the task at hand. There is also the hope that the therapist, teacher, or author will have some special wisdom on the topic of discussion.

But this is most evident in the dyadic roles of parent and child. In a family group it is the role of the parents to be wise, and the role of the children to be less wise but obedient. Or the role of the older brother to be wise and the role of the younger brother to be less so, but learning. That works well when the role is a good match for the person filling it. But if the older family members have the role of being wise without the substance, if they are acting the part, then, strange as it may sound, they may make it easy for the younger brother to take the role of being a troublemaker. Then when they look at him, they feel wise by comparison.

In group psychology, this troublemaker is called a scapegoat, borrowing the biblical term. The Church teaches, as we said above, that we all carry a complex inheritance of good and bad in ourselves. A little self-reflection shows that at any given moment, we may be more conscious of one aspect or the other. If the group members as a whole wish to feel good about themselves, they can disown any awareness of the bad, focusing this awareness on a scapegoat within the group or some outcast group. This allows the members to have a fragile sense of their goodness and superiority. They criticize the scapegoat or outcast group, but "vehemently resist" their "attempts to become good" because once that happens, they will have to wake up to their own mixed state of being good and bad or find another scapegoat or outcast group (Smith & Berg, 1997, p. 70).

Here's the crux of it: In the complex life of a family group or, say, a church group, there may be wayward members in need of repentance—people who are ever on the prayer list and the gossip list—who are, nevertheless, counted on to fulfill their role of being "bad." And the good people—people who, as a group, are represented by the older son—may deplore how these members are, but at least they can be counted on to fulfill their role. However problematic these issues may be, problem drinking, drugging, overspending, belligerence, and so on become features of the social landscape. Others adjust around the issues and know what is expected of them. People settle into their complementary roles of being rescuers, disciplinarians, helpers, and so on.

The amazing thing about group life is that when people finally start to get better, they are usually bombarded with messages to change back to what they were (see Lerner, 1985). Now in our Orthodox faith this is normally spoken of as a manifestation of the envy of the demons, and so it is. The envious demons often act through unsuspecting people of good will. The very people who wanted the "prodigals" to change get angry with them. So using the older brother as a metaphor for the better functioning members of the family or group, in order to answer the question of whether the Prodigal's older brother can forgive and welcome him home, we need to look at his role, his attitude, and his anger as part of the life of the group. Again, we will weave back and forth between the characters and story line of the parable on the one hand, and our reflection on group life on the other.

The older brother

What was the older brother's relationship with the younger brother while he was gone? Was he indifferent? I highly doubt it. The two of them were flesh and blood and a piece of him went missing when his brother left—how could he not think about him? Perhaps he prayed for him to change, but what would that change look like? A full reinstatement in the family seemed out of the question—the boy had committed irreversible deeds. Perhaps he even hoped for the boy to be punished to make up for the family honor. He possibly had to do more work around the farm to make up for his brother's absence. He probably resented that. Perhaps he felt enhanced pride and self-esteem regarding his faithfulness to the father, now much more obvious because of the transgressions of the younger boy. Perhaps he looked with some hidden envy at his brother's freedom, but did not dare acknowledge this to himself or anyone else.

So why did he get furious? First let me remind you that the father in the parable has always been understood to be our Heavenly Father. Without losing sight of that dimension, the original hearers of the parable were expecting to hear a description of a familiar, Jewish father. They would expect that the good father in the parable had given both his sons words of admonishment and correction during their growing years. They might suspect that the younger son had shown signs of a rebellious nature early on. They all knew the law, and by Jewish law, the father had every right to have his son stoned if he refused to listen to admonishment. The Book of Deuteronomy spells this out clearly (21:18–21).

Perhaps the original hearers were expecting the younger son to be summarily denounced when he arrived back home, without a chance to even plead his case. They, reflected in the older brother who embodied their attitudes, were the same men who wanted to stone the woman caught in adultery (see Jn. 8:4–11). Their righteousness was proved by their willingness to uphold the disciplinary codes of the law so that the people would not be corrupted by bad influences.

So I think the Prodigal showed great courage in coming home, knowing that he perhaps deserved to die. He, in asking to be like one of the hired servants, accepted the death of his sonship in order to preserve at least some relationship with his father—this was life. Of course the older brother did not witness the Prodigal's secret confession of sin before the father; his sense of justice was outraged on various counts.

What else can we say about the older son's anger? It flared up quickly. In order for his ire to kindle he had to make a snap judgment that here was a wrongful situation that threatened his sense of what was right and sacred. He had to blame some-one. If he really loved and trusted his father he might have thought— "What's going on—I'm all turned around—I've got to ask Dad about it." Instead he judged his father: "From knee high I've been told that if a boy is disobedient to his parents they would have him stoned to death. I've really tried to be good and obedient so this wouldn't happen to me. It's really been hard work for me to be so good—to bite my tongue when I wanted to answer back. To labor in the hot fields when I was tired. If this brother of mine can do such outrageous things and be received back with honor, it's a slap in the face to me. It says that all my hard work and efforts to be good were mean-ingless. I should have done like my brother." To flare up as quickly as he did, it helps to have a store of unexpressed re-sentments.

The Return of the "Prodigal"

The return of the "prodigal" in the family setting

WHAT DOES IT LOOK LIKE in the family setting when the "prodigal" returns? Perhaps a child has run away from home and is involved in drugs—the family is dealing with very complex issues. They may deny and minimize the trouble the child is in. They may be afraid to talk with one another at all. Or they may rally together over the loss and forget their individual differences over smaller issues in order to deal with this major threat. Sometimes parents with a stormy marriage will reconcile so they can focus together on a problem child. On some level they seem to have needed the child to have problems so they could bury their differences. But as long as they persist in projecting all their badness into the youngster how will they get along if the "prodigal" returns and repents?

It's fallen human nature to want to be in a better place without having to do the work that it takes to get there—to feel better without doing better. If we see someone surpass us we want what they have without the suffering and sacrifice it took for them to get there. This, of course, produces terrible envy. And envy tries its hardest to drag others down to its level. Some family members, from this position of envy, will reintroduce the returned "prodigal" to drugs and alcohol. Some will bait and badger this person, hoping to produce

71

angry outbursts so as to confirm, at least in their own minds, that the repentance is fake.

Perhaps this example sounds extreme—hopefully these issues will never touch you or your family. But extreme examples often help us see everyday issues more clearly, just as in the original parable. Nowadays, youngsters in juvenile detention often say that their parents' fighting was a major reason they ran from home and got into trouble with sex, drugs, and the law. Some of them really repent in the juvenile facility—they take to heart all they learn in classes on drug addiction and relapse prevention, social skills, anger management, positive thinking and so on. What happens when they get back home? Sometimes the family members, whose fragile sense of goodness depended on looking down on the family troublemaker, have to deal with a shocking upset—the former problem child has learned life skills that they don't have. The returned "prodigal" is talking a new language, preaching values and principles that the parents may not have been exposed to.

The family is used to using familiar scripts when they fight. They say: "You're to blame because you never listen to me!" and "You're to blame because you always do the same old thing!" "What's the matter with you!" The returned "prodigal" comes back saying "We need to stop blaming each other—we need to make 'I' statements instead. 'When you do this I feel hurt and upset.' When someone upsets us we need to stop pretending to mind-read and ask them what they really meant." How is that going to go over with the parents? Maybe they're going to wonder who this upstart is that's correcting them and telling them how to fight. Instead of forgiving the returned "prodigal" for the past and being able to welcome a new source of healing for the whole family, they'll continue to label the child as a troublemaker—only now, a troublemaker of a different sort.

This different sort of troublemaker is arousing in them feelings of shame and inadequacy by showing them a higher way when it's not the youngster's role to be wise. The parents feel their role being usurped and resent it. Back to our parable, the Lord was correcting this tendency to identify with the role, rather than the qualities, of leadership and the tendency to resist learning from a person of low status. Love and humility are wanted here. He might have said to the big brother, *Therefore I tell you,* your *brother's sins, which are many, are forgiven; for he loved much: but the one who is forgiven little, loves little* (cf: Lk. 7:47).

The return of the "prodigal" in the civic sphere

WHAT DOES IT LOOK LIKE in the civic sphere when the "prodigal" returns? It may look like a citizen trying to reenter society from the criminal justice system. In an age when more and more employers are demanding a criminal background check, this gets harder and harder. It is hard for these "prodigals" to find work and housing. Communities monitor sexual offenders in their midst. Is this wrong? I am not trying to pass judgment on complex issues, but rather, to look at how we find ourselves part of groups that make it hard for the returning "prodigal" to be forgiven and received.

Many of our mentally ill end up in prisons because they lack access to the help they need before their illness gets them into legal trouble. After release there are obstacles to obtaining mental health services: Community clinics may be reluctant to accept patients with a conviction record. Any government health care benefits will have been discontinued during incarceration and have to be reapplied for upon release. This can mean a critical lapse in stabilizing medications. So mental illness leads to incarceration, and a history of incarceration impedes access to mental health services.

Of course we all know that some returning "prodigals" have made a permanent change in their lives, and others will go back to their old ways. Or again, some may have to go and return a few times before they stay. One of the dilemmas is that people see their own group close up, in detail, with individual members identified and distinguished from one another. People see others' groups from afar as a conglomerate, and everyone looks the same (see Schneider, 2005). In biblical times, it is precisely because the Pharisees kept their skirts clean—never associated or shared a meal with evil-doers and transgressors—that the sinners all looked alike. Perhaps some will make a genuine repentance and it will stick, while others will "backslide," but how do they know whom to trust if they never associate and all sinners look the same? So the "older brothers," whether as Pharisees then or as law-abiding citizens now, have a difficult trust issue and tend to resolve it by trusting no one outside their group.

What does the "older brother's" repentance and willingness to forgive look like in the civic sphere? We could further educate ourselves about mental illness and become more aware of prejudicial attitudes toward the mentally ill. Progress might manifest as financial support for mental health ministries and other humanizing programs. Two very good national programs are the National Alliance on Mental Illness (NAMI) and the Fellowship of Orthodox Christians United to Serve (FOCUS North America). It could look like advocacy for the mentally ill to receive the help they need and deserve. Again, it might mean a heightened awareness and interest in prison mentoring programs, or in mentoring for newly released prisoners. It is through mentoring that prisoners become known as individuals, trusting relationships can be developed with law-abiding citizens, and the "prodigals," when they are released, are able to have character witnesses when they apply for work and housing.

The return of the "prodigal" in the church setting

WHAT DOES IT LOOK LIKE in a parish setting when the "prodigal" returns? It may look like an established congregation being asked to open its arms to an inquirer who is known to have been an evil-doer—a transgressor. The congregation, like the older brother, does not witness the private repentance in the "prodigal's" heart. There is mistrust and suspicion—is this person sincere? Do I want this individual around my children? This is not an easy situation because we know the odds—many people relapse and return to their former ways.

In this case, the pastor might represent the father figure in our parable. The pastor would discern the "prodigal's" readiness for change and admission to the Eucharistic Feast. The "older brother" is represented by the parish as a group. How are known and reformed evil-doers received? Will people associate with the "prodigals"? Will they sit or stand next to them in the worship and show them how to follow the service? Will they invite them to their table at coffee hour? Will some begin to feel that they don't want their families to be part of a congregation that receives such people and begin to search for another church? Both responses are understandable as forgiveness and reinstatement are not the same thing as full trust. Trust must be earned.

In circumstances like these, the "older brother," as the established congregation, may forgive the one whom God has forgiven, being humble enough to say "there, but for God's providence, go I." When they compare their lives with the "prodigal's" they see their own sins as even greater given the greater advantages in life they also enjoyed.

Then again, the "prodigal" may return in the guise of those who were born into the faith but saw it as a token of their cultural heritage rather than living as committed members of a faith community. Will they be embraced when they return to parish life, or feel like outsiders? Will the "older brother" recognize himself in the parable and, like King David, turn his anger against his own hidden sins? Will he escort the returnees to the Eucharistic Feast?

Summary

WE HAVE LOOKED AT the scene of the "prodigal's" return from many social angles: the delinquent child returning to the family, the prisoner returning to society, the sinner or lapsed member turning to the Church. We have looked at how the big brother's attitudes of anger and suspicion may be recapitulated in groups to which we belong: the family, society at large, and the parish group. We have seen how, when people are playing the role of parent, concerned citizen, or spiritual leader—without developing the substance, the qualities that these roles demand—they tend to count on the presence of outcasts in society so that they can prove themselves superior by comparison. But humility demands that we compare ourselves with those above us, with the saints, so that we begin to realize that we, too, are just beginners.

For the big brother to repent and forgive, he needs the law of love. When he thinks of his still-missing brother he must think, in the words of Elder Porphyrios:

> We are one even with those who are not close to the Church. They are distant on account of ignorance. We must pray that God will enlighten them and change them so that they too may come to Christ [SHCC, 2005, p. 89].

When he hears the music and dancing, and the servant tells him that his long lost brother has returned he must feel deeply that he does not "wish to be saved alone and without all others being saved" (p. 89). As he stands outside the door, he remembers that "When we set ourselves apart from others, we are not Christians" (p. 89). The Pharisee must move from being set apart from others to being set apart from the sin within him — from "inheritance of the evil that exists in the world from Adam until the present" (p. 134). He must remember that:

> The important thing is for us to enter the Church — to unite ourselves with our fellow men, with the joys and sorrows of each and everyone, to feel that they are our own, to pray for everyone, to have care for their salvation, to forget about ourselves, to do everything for them just as Christ did for us [p. 88].

Then he goes into the Eucharistic Feast, rejoicing with his Heavenly Father and his resurrected brother.

In conclusion

I HOPE YOU WILL CONTINUE to contemplate the character of the older son in the parable of the Prodigal. Yes, there is a bit of the older son, a little bit of the Pharisee in all of us — trusting in our own righteousness, our own visible deeds, saying "thank God I am not like other people — thieves, crooks, immoral, or even like this so-called brother of mine." And more than that, just as the Jewish sages and Pharisees threatened ostracism from the group to any member who supported Jesus and His reception of sinners, we find ourselves part of groups where it is unpopular to welcome returning "prodigals" with open arms. These groups look on the "prodigal" with suspicion, unable to discern the difference between the truly repentant and the manipulator because they are too busy to notice these outsiders. Or, as in the portrayal of the Pharisees, they may be so busy keeping their own skirts clean and their own self-esteem polished that they don't care to get to know "those people."

If we suspect this to be the case how can we, as individuals, make a difference in our family, religious, social, and civic groups? As always, change begins with self, the only person we can really change. I invite you to think for a moment of one person in your life who seems to be in need of major life healing, of repentance, of a return to the Father. If this were to miraculously happen today, how might that make your life harder as well as easier? What might it be like to have this person enter as a more equal partner in your shared relationships? What might you lose in terms of power and status in your group if this person had a more equal voice? How might you have to focus on your own problems rather than on theirs? What might you see in yourself if free to do this self-examination?

If even one person in a group can hold onto the ambiguities, the pluses and the minuses, and resist an us-them mentality, it can go a long way in helping the group as a whole to accept the ambiguities (see Smith & Berg, 1997). It can help the group as a whole to accept that all the members, even the best functioning ones, have issues to work on, sins to repent of. It can help the group as a whole to see that the returning "prodigals" never lost the image of the heavenly Father in the depths of the soul and that now the buried image is being renewed. The older brother can extend forgiveness to the younger and together they can approach the Father saying, "Be merciful to me a sinner!"

Glory be to God!

References and Bibliography
Third Essay

Danker, Frederick W. (Ed.). (2000). *A Greek-English lexicon of the New Testament and other early Christian literature*, 3rd ed. Chicago: University of Chicago.

Douglas, James D. (1974). *The new international dictionary of the Christian Church*. Grand Rapids, MI: Zondervan.

Holy Apostles Convent & Dormition Skete. (2003). *The Orthodox New Testament*, vol. 1. Buena Vista, CO: Holy Apostles Convent & Dormition Skete.

Lerner, Harriet G. (1985). *The dance of anger: A woman's guide to changing the patterns of intimate relationships*. New York: Harper & Row.

Oden, Thomas C. (Gen. Ed.). (2003). *Ancient Christian commentary on Scripture. New Testament*, vol. 8, (A. A. Just, Jr., Ed.). Downers Grove, IL: InterVarsity.

Pavle of Serbia, (Patriarch). (2017). *Life according to the Gospel* (A. Petrović, Trans.). Alhambra, CA: Sebastian.

Schneider, David J. (2005). *The psychology of stereotyping*. New York: Guilford.

Sisters of the Holy Convent of Chrysopigi (SHCC), (Eds.). (2005). *Wounded by love: The life and the wisdom of Elder Porphyrios*. Limni, Evia, Greece: Denise Harvey.

Smith, Kenwyn & Berg, David. (1997). *Paradoxes of group life: Understanding conflict, paralysis, and movement in group dynamics*. San Francisco: Jossey-Bass.

Theophylact, St. (1997). *The explanation by Blessed Theophylact of the Holy Gospel according to St. Luke*. (Fr. C. Stade, Trans.). House Springs, MO: Chrysostom.

Vasileios, (Archimandrite). (1995). "The parable of the prodigal son." *Epiphany Journal 15* (2 & 3), 49–60.

Printed in Great Britain
by Amazon

16139528R00058